☆ THE FILMS OF ☆

Ronald Reagan

BOOKS BY TONY THOMAS

The Films of Errol Flynn (with Rudy Behlmer and Clifford McCarty)

Ustinov in Focus

The Films of Kirk Douglas

The Busby Berkeley Book

Music for the Movies

The Films of Marlon Brando

Cads and Cavaliers

Song and Dance Man: The Films of Gene Kelly

Burt Lancaster

The Films of the Forties

Hollywood's Hollywood (with Rudy Behlmer)

Gregory Peck

Harry Warren and the Hollywood Musical

The Great Adventure Films

The Films of 20th Century-Fox (with Aubrey Solomon)

Film Score

From a Life of Adventure (The Writings of Errol Flynn)

☆ THE FILMS OF ☆
Ronald Reagan

by Tony Thomas

CITADEL PRESS · Secaucus, N. J.

First edition

Copyright © 1980 by Tony Thomas
All rights reserved
Published by Citadel Press
A division of Lyle Stuart Inc.
120 Enterprise Ave., Secaucus, N.J. 07094
In Canada: General Publishing Co. Limited
Don Mills, Ontario
Manufactured in the United States of America by
Halliday Lithograph, West Hanover, Mass.

Designed by Dennis J. Grastorf

Library of Congress Cataloging in Publication Data

Thomas, Tony, 1927-
    The films of Ronald Reagan.

    1. Reagan, Ronald.   I.   Title.
PN2287.R25T47   791.43'028'094   80-20850
ISBN 0-8065-0751-9

For Suzy

☆☆☆

Acknowledgments

MY PRIMARY THANKS go to the gentleman who is the subject of this book for the use of the tape recordings I did with him and for permission to quote from his autobiography *Where's the Rest of Me?*, written with Richard G. Hubler and published by Duell, Sloan and Pearce, New York, 1965. Most of the research on the films was done in the library of The Academy of Motion Picture Arts and Sciences (Los Angeles), and for that I am grateful to Mrs. Terry Roach and her staff. In the all important and difficult job of illustrating this book I am especially grateful to Mark Ricci of The Memory Shop (New York). In that regard my thanks also go to Eddie Brandt and Mike Hawks of Saturday Matinee (North Hollywood); Bob Colman of the Hollywood Poster Exchange (Los Angeles); Gunnard Nelson; Robert Knutson, the director of the Special Collections Division of the University of Southern California (Los Angeles); George Pratt of the Eastman House (Rochester); and Maxine Fleckner, the director of Film Archives of the Wisconsin Center for Film and Theatre Research. Quite obviously, books of this kind cannot be done without such cooperation. I am deeply grateful for the help of those here listed.

Tony Thomas

☆☆☆

The Films of Ronald Reagan

Ronald Reagan—Star Politico

IN 1966, not long before he took office as the governor of California, I was assigned by my then employers, the Canadian Broadcasting Corporation, to tape a series of interviews with Ronald Reagan for the CBC Radio Network. The focal point of the interviews was to be the character of the man, not his political leanings. I had by this time interviewed a great many Hollywood luminaries and learned never to take their images for granted. A few were more interesting in person but many were far less so. In the case of Ronald Reagan, it was not simply a matter of him being more interesting, but of the man having substantial knowledge, and an ability to discuss his views with more conviction than his film performances would suggest. Like many other people, I had enjoyed his work on screen and I shared the general view that he was a good, likable, workaday actor, although not one of any distinction. But Reagan had, by 1966, been making movies for thirty years, and no actor lasts that long without both ability and stamina.

My curiosity about interviewing Reagan was whetted a few months earlier when I had taped a CBC interview with Barry Goldwater in Phoenix, Arizona. I asked Goldwater for his opinion of the governor-elect of California, and since they were friends and fellow Republicans, I expected to hear praise, but I was not prepared for the calmly convincing manner in which Mr. Goldwater stated his views. He said, in so many measured words, that Ronald Reagan was a natural-born politician with a remarkable grasp of human conditions, and that he would doubtless become a very successful man in American politics. Later, in Hollywood, I asked the same question of several people who had known Reagan for a long time and they agreed with Mr. Goldwater. I learned that Reagan had been a formidable union administrator, and in a few opinions, the best president the Screen Actors Guild ever

had. Outside of Hollywood there were many who were amazed that an actor could become a successful politician, but an actress who had known Reagan since his earliest days in the movies said, "He's always been a politician, even if he didn't know it. He just happened to spend a number of years making a living as an actor."

I was not qualified to question Ronald Reagan very deeply about his political platform, but because I was planning to become a permanent resident of the state of which he was to become governor, I was curious to learn something about his nature. My main interest, as an almost congenital film buff, was to hear him talk about the "good old days" of the picture business. He had joined Warner Bros. in 1937, in its heyday, and had worked with all their famed players—Bette Davis, James Cagney, Errol Flynn, Dick Powell, Humphrey Bogart, Olivia de Havilland, Pat O'Brien, and the rest. It was an indulgence for me to discuss those times and the stars, and I was being paid by the CBC to do it! I asked Reagan about his views on the film industry at that time and found that they were ones largely of regret. He disliked the lack of control within Hollywood. "In those pre-war days we had the contract system. The studios employed not only stars and writers and directors on a permanent basis but all kinds of technicians, so there was a stability to the business. Today it's a hungry scramble. Now it's a case of everybody waiting for the phone to ring to get a job."

What particularly pained Ronald Reagan, as we spoke about Hollywood during that first interview —and it is a pain that has increased greatly since that time—was the moral decline of the industry in regard to dealing with sleazy, vulgar material and foisting it upon the public. "In those days if a problem came up that concerned the whole industry there was a phone number you could call. With that

9

one call you could arrange a meeting of all your heads of guilds and unions and studio management to determine policy. You could address them all for the good of the industry. Today there is no such phone number, and there's not much you can do about rallying the industry.''

That an actor should enter the field of politics did not seem outlandish to Ronald Reagan. ''Recognizing your responsibility in public affairs is the equipment of any man, including an actor. You come to a moment when you feel you have a call to face responsibility. I've always believed you have to pay your way in the world. This is in contrast to the man who goes into politics because it looks like an exciting life or a good living. The actor who finds himself facing this kind of responsibility has this much going for him—no one can accuse him of doing it for personal gain. We already have a life that offers more variety and enjoyment than most, and we don't have the headaches that go with politics.''

The common theory that an actor can be a deceiver as a politician because of his performing ability does not hold much water with Reagan. ''The television close-up is more revealing than when an audience only saw a speaker on the platform. Only those in the front row saw him up close. To the others he was just a small figure on a platform. When the camera comes in on a close-up the speaker had better be honest and mean what he says. Honesty comes through, and vice versa.''

* * *

Ronald Wilson Reagan was born in the tiny town of Tampico, Illinois, on February 6, 1911. He was the second of the two sons (no daughters) of John Edward Reagan and his wife Nelle (Wilson). Ronald's brother Neil had been born two years previously. Reagan senior, known to all as Jack, was a first-generation, black-haired Catholic Irishman who made his living as a shoe salesman, and whose experience as such ranged from being a clerk in a variety of stores to at times managing his own business. Jack Reagan took a serious interest in footwear and was considered to be good at his trade. The one apparent blemish in his character was a propensity for whisky, which left his youngest son with a lifelong dislike for alcohol. The occasional sight of Reagan's father ''under the influence'' appears to be the only major upsetting factor in a childhood which his contemporaries describe as being ''about as traumatic as apple pie.''

Baby Ronald.

The Reagans were a nice, ordinary, Midwest working-class family who adhered to the simple basics of American life and who were never involved in events either tragic or scandalous. Nelle Reagan was a Protestant of Scots-English stock, a lady sympathetic to her husband's weakness for drink but morally opposed to it, whose interests in literature and the arts provided a family counterbalance to his bluff and gregarious nature. Jack Reagan taught his sons to stand up for themselves in life, to fight fair whenever a fight was unavoidable, to respect the rights of the working man and to support the Democratic party.

Three-year-old Ronald, with brother Neil and parents.

10

The first nine years in the life of Ronald Reagan were spent in a number of residences in Illinois. His father took jobs wherever they were available and the Reagans did not own a home until many years later, when their son became a well-employed actor and bought the family a house in California. They lived for periods in Tampico, the south side of Chicago, Galesburg, Monmouth and again in Tampico before settling in Dixon, a town of ten thousand population about ninety miles from Chicago. It is Dixon which Reagan fondly regards as his hometown and the setting of a life which he describes as being Tom Sawyer-like, without the outlandish adventures of Twain's imagination.

Stars of the Eureka College football team in 1930.

A thoughtful young Ronald, on the left end of the second row, at school in Tampico, Illinois.

Reagan inherited a hale and hearty personality from his father, along with a certain amount of anger over the foibles of the world. Reagan senior possessed a wry sense of humor. He enjoyed telling jokes and was appreciated by his friends and customers as a good raconteur. He had the Irish "gift of gab" and it would be difficult for his famous son to deny a similar characteristic. He was also a man with a great desire for success, who never found it, except vicariously, in his actor son. Jack Reagan did not live to see his son enter politics, but it doubtless would have pleased him greatly.

Young Ronald was undersized as a boy, but wiry and energetic. He was fond of the outdoor life and hunting, fishing, swimming in creeks, trekking through woods and climbing hills took up most of his out-of-school attention. He also had a marked love of sports, although this was somewhat curtailed by a case of shortsightedness which ruled out

baseball but not football. Reagan became adept at this game at an early age, which had considerable bearing on his later professional life. He recalls a passion for charging down makeshift football fields with motley gangs of boys, resulting in endless cuts and bruises, but states that these were the happiest times of his life.

His school work was above average and he abetted his learning with long hours of reading in the public library, to cater to his curiosity about the world. His mother fostered an early interest in literature and often gave dramatic readings in her home and at social gatherings at which young Ronald was badgered into participating. He was taken to the performances of visiting drama companies to see

Reagan, the college footballer.

fifth-rate versions of famous plays, but this exposure was enough to increase his interest in the people who went on stage and emoted. However, attending plays was less pleasurable than going to the movies and cheering the antics of such renowned celluloid heroes as Douglas Fairbanks, Tom Mix and William S. Hart.

In the summer of 1925, fourteen-year-old Ronald was forced to relinquish some of the hours he devoted to football to take his first job. The Reagan family income was always uncertain, and it became necessary for the boy to help the common cause, as well as to save money for his own further education. He joined a construction company and went to work with a pick and shovel ten hours a day. By the end of the summer he had been able to save two hundred dollars. The following summer he took a more likable job as a lifeguard at Dixon's Lowell Park, which he continued to work at as a summer job for the next seven years. This position afforded him exercise and fresh air and gave him his first real sense of the nature of human beings, particularly in regard to gratitude. Reagan discovered that people did not enjoy being rescued, and that they invariably did not believe they needed rescuing and that saving their lives in view of others caused them painful embarrassment. But the job was better than digging foundation ditches.

The lifeguard of Lowell Park, 1931.

One of the people Reagan most admired during his teens was a high school footballer named Garland Waggoner. When Waggoner became a star player at Eureka College, Reagan decided that it would be his school as well. Eureka was a Christian church college similar to Texas Christian University, but a fraction the size. The school was co-educational and had facilities for about 250 students. It was situated about twenty miles from Peoria and was a college with minuscule funds, honorable traditions and high standards. Reagan enrolled in the fall of 1928 and became very fond of the school. He states in his autobiography, "I still think, after years of crisscrossing the United States, that it is one of the loveliest colleges in existence. It seemed to me then, as I walked up the path, to be another home. There were five big main buildings, arranged in a semicircle, built of red brick with white-framed windows, a style that is an American reminiscence of English Georgian architecture. Walls were covered with friendly ivy, and the whole framed with huge elms and rolling green lawns."

Reagan did not have sufficient funds to enroll at Eureka. The tuition was $180 a year and his total savings came to only about twice that amount. But sympathetic school officials, no doubt sensing his desperation and longing, awarded him a scholarship at half tuition costs and a job to enable him to work his way through college. Reagan washed dishes, served as a lifeguard at the college pool and as a coach in sports events. In addition to being a conscientious student, he took advantage of the college standing in the scholastic football league to excel at his favorite sport.

Something occurred at Eureka that would reveal a facet of Reagan's nature not previously shown—a propensity for political discussions and debates. The college, always strapped for funds, made the decision to take drastic measures to curb expenditures and revise the management. These plans would have reduced the number of faculty and deprived many students of their studies. The instigating president persuaded the school board to adopt his plans, overlooking the reaction of the student body, which, at a school with a strong family environment, was virtually fascistic. The students went on strike and Reagan was foremost among the organizers. He was a representative of the freshman class and was partly responsible for the highly organized, orderly petitions made to the school board. Students and teachers stood united in their cause

The sportscaster of Radio Station WHO, Des Moines, 1933.

and soon defeated the plans of the new president. It was during this time that Reagan first stood before an audience and addressed them with his views. He discovered the thrill of holding the attention of a group.

The pride of the Midwest airwaves, 1934.

While at Eureka Reagan again became involved in the business of play acting. During a summer vacation in Dixon he had seen the touring company production of *Journey's End* and reacted to it with curiosity about the job of an actor. Theatrical drama appealed to him, and he joined the school's dramatic society. He had previously performed in plays at the Dixon High School, but now it seemed an interest worth further consideration. By the time of graduation, young Reagan was undecided about his main pursuit—sports or drama. His passion for both had to do, he admits, with a love of showing off. Either profession seemed an exciting way to live for a boy who had grown up wearing his brother's castoffs, whose father struggled to make fifty dollars a week and whose mother had to work to supplement the family income.

The first publicity portrait of Ronald Reagan at Warners in 1937. Note the hair is no longer parted in the middle.

The Eureka Dramatic Society won second place in 1931 in the annual play contest staged by Northwestern University, and Ronald Reagan was one of a half dozen student actors awarded an honors trophy. The following year when the initial euphoria of attending Eureka wore off, Reagan decided that he wanted to participate in some form of show business. Hollywood and Broadway were too far removed from reality to consider, but he possessed a talent that could possibly get him into radio broadcasting—the knack of ad-libbing sports commentary.

13

When Reagan left Eureka with a Bachelor of Arts degree and credits in sociology and economics, he raised eyebrows by claiming that he could earn five thousand dollars a year within five years. It was a boast, but one that actually materialized. In the late summer of 1932, he left for Chicago, at that time, a major center of American radio, and went about breaking into the business of microphones and airwaves. NBC was his first point of attack, then CBS, then the big independent stations and finally the stations listed in the telephone book. Since he had no money, Reagan made the rounds mostly on foot. With refusals at every point, he decided to take a second crack at NBC. It was impossible to see anyone on the managerial level, not to mention get an audition, but a kindly secretary was impressed enough to give him advice. She said there wasn't a chance of anyone without experience breaking into

broadcasting at that level, but that there were many smaller stations always looking for talent.

The weary Reagan hitchhiked back to Dixon. His father perked up his spirits with a suggested plan, which was to take the family car and map out a few days of driving within a certain radius to hit all the stations possible. The first "hit" Reagan made was WOC, Davenport, Iowa, a station which derived its call letters from its parent company, World of Chiropractic, founded by Colonel B. J. Palmer of the Palmer School of Chiropractic. The colonel also owned station WHO, Des Moines, and both stations had a large listening audience. It was unlikely that a newcomer could break into radio even on this level, but that is precisely what Ronald Reagan did.

His mentor in broadcasting was Peter MacArthur, a gruff but warm-hearted Scotsman who had come to America as a member of Harry Lauder's

A poolside shot from the late 1930s.

15

troupe of vaudevillians, but who had given up the life of an entertainer when his arthritis reached a crippling degree. MacArthur had gone to the Palmer School of Chiropractic seeking relief from his pains, but because of his fine speaking voice and expressive manner he was hired by their radio department. He was program director of WOC when the eager young Reagan approached him for a job. MacArthur explained that he was a week late for the auditions they had been conducting for a new announcer. This infuriating piece of news caused Reagan to storm out of the office, shouting, "How the hell does a guy ever get to be a sports announcer if he can't get inside a station?"

The use of the term 'sports announcer' was responsible for Reagan's start in radio. MacArthur called him back and demanded to know if he knew anything about football, and if he did, could he do play-by-play commentary? When Reagan replied affirmatively, MacArthur steered him into an empty studio and instructed him to demonstrate. Reagan recalled the exciting fourth quarter of a game Eu-

reka had played opposite Western State University and launched into twenty minutes of frenzied description. MacArthur was so impressed that he told Reagan to return in a few days and take a crack at being the announcer for a football broadcast—for five dollars and car fare. Reagan's first words on the air were, "How do you do, ladies and gentlemen. We are speaking to you from high atop the Memorial Stadium of the University of Iowa, looking down from the west on the south forty-yard line . . ." His natural talent for announcer's patter and his enthusiasm and knowledge of football caused him to be hired for a subsequent game broadcast. When an opening at the station became available, he was signed on at WOC at a salary of one hundred dollars a month—a seeming elevation from poverty to wealth.

Despite his skill at sports patter, Reagan was not considered a good announcer in the regular line of work. He had difficulty reading scripts, at getting the words 'off the paper,' and this problem stayed with him even as a movie actor. First read-throughs

Ronald Reagan and his fiancée, Jane Wyman, snapped at a San Francisco restaurant in November, 1939.

of scripts would cause directors and fellow actors in his early Hollywood days to question his screen ability. But once Reagan learned his lines, he always did well. In those first few months at WOC, though, several sponsors complained about the mediocre manner in which their commercials were being read, and on one occasion Reagan was fired by the station. (He was rehired when his replacement refused to accept the terms of employment.) Reagan put more effort into his work.

Peter MacArthur again gave Reagan a push in the right career direction. When station WHO in Des Moines needed an announcer for sports events, MacArthur sent Reagan, and over the next four years he built a first class reputation in this specialized area of broadcasting. WHO was a 50,000 watt station with a huge audience throughout the Midwest. When it became a part of the NBC network, Reagan was heard coast-to-coast on many top sports broadcasts. He announced dozens of football games from major press boxes in the Midwest and covered hundreds of big league baseball games,

track events and swimming meets. He was also occasionally hired to write sports columns in newspapers and to address audiences at banquets. Ronald Reagan found himself well-employed and thoroughly enjoying life.

Reagan's full-time employment in radio had begun in January of 1933, when Franklin Delano Roosevelt came to presidential power. To his Democrat family, this seemed like the best of coincidences. His father had happily accepted a position as an official with the Works Progress Administration. Jack Reagan was respected for his sympathetic aid to fellow citizens in Dixon, Illinois, and this post also gave his broadcaster son more insight into the world of politics. Sadly, Ronald's father shortly thereafter became afflicted with a heart condition.

It was at this time that Ronald Reagan indulged himself in a lifelong hankering to ride horses. This desire might have had its start with the idolized cowboy stars in the movies, but it was also evidence of Reagan's love of sports, the outdoors and being in motion. A fellow announcer was a reserve

Wedding day—January 26, 1940, with Reagan's parents, Nelle and Jack.

officer in the cavalry and suggested that Reagan apply for a commission, giving him access to army horses and all the free riding he could want. The idea appealed to Reagan until he learned that eyesight was of primary importance in the commissioning of a cavalry officer. Reagan at this time wore glasses, and would later wear corneal lenses once they became available. But in 1935 he became a reserve second lieutenant with the 14th Cavalry Regiment at Des Moines by the simple expedient of cheating. During his medical examination, instead of a piece of cardboard, he held his hands over his deficient eyes and peeped through the slight gaps between his fingers. This had the same effect as punching a pinhole in a cardboard, producing the effect of a corrective lens for a nearsighted person.

As Reagan's fame as a sports announcer grew, he began the first of several annual trips to California's Catalina Island to report on the spring training of the Chicago Cubs. He rarely had an opportunity to get away in the busy summer months, so the trips to the coast allowed a welcome break from the severe Iowa winters. Reagan had not forgotten his idea of breaking into theatrical life. In school and college, and with encouragement from his mother, he enjoyed dramatic performing. Being a sports commentator had satisfied some of that hunger, but during a visit to California in February of 1937, he decided to take measures to get into the movies.

The luck and the ease with which Reagan entered radio were repeated in his Hollywood approach. Joy Hodges, a singer Reagan knew in Des Moines, was then singing with Jimmy Grier's Orchestra at the Biltmore Bowl in Los Angeles. When Reagan asked her advice, she arranged for him to meet agent Bill Meiklejohn, who was sufficiently impressed to ask for a screentest at Warner Bros. for the hopeful. The casting director, Max Arnow, agreed to the test, at which Reagan acted a scene from the Philip Barry play *Holiday*. When he was asked to wait in Los Angeles for a few days until Jack Warner had a chance to view the test, Reagan replied that he had to return to Des Moines and his job, an independent manner that probably prompted the telegram from Warners offering a seven year contract and a starting wage of two hundred dollars a week.

Ronald Reagan's Hollywood career began on June 1, 1937. Rumor had it that young contract actors could languish around the studio for weeks and possibly months before being called before the cameras. But Reagan was assigned the lead in a

With Laraine Day at MGM in 1941, checking the script while making "The Bad Man."

minor picture within days of being on the lot, and was thereafter kept busy by Warners for most of the time he was in their employ, especially during the early years of his contract. He was somewhat surprised at his easy entry into the picture business, assuming that there were multitudes of young men of his kind available. In fact, Warners needed a likable male actor in his mid-twenties, with typical good American looks—a type that Reagan fitted perfectly. The studio had just lost the actor Ross Alexander (a suicide) and Reagan resembled him enough to take his place. They were particularly impressed by Reagan's speaking voice and his bright, enthusiastic personality.

Reagan's debut on the screen was ironic in that the studio cast him as a rather brash radio announcer in *Love Is on the Air*. That same pleasantly eager quality became the keynote of his movie image over the next few years. Reagan found that scooping up the lead in his first film was no guarantee of immediate stardom and that he was strictly a journeyman actor to his employers, whereas other studios might have spent time grooming him as a star. Warner Bros., often described as a "working class" studio, was run like a well-tooled factory, ever conscious of budgets and rarely sympathetic

Captain Ronald Reagan, United States Army Air Corps, lunching with brother Neil in 1944.

toward employees. This toughness had, in fact, been largely responsible for the growth of trade unionism in Hollywood. The elation of playing the lead in *Love Is on the Air* was soon lessened by Reagan's receiving an unbilled bit part in his next film, *Hollywood Hotel,* and by having his small role in *Submarine D-1* cut from the final print. He hardly had time to dwell on any disappointments, though.

In 1938 he appeared in no fewer than eight movies, ranging from leads in B pictures to small roles in A products. It was a year in which he quickly learned the techniques of acting before cameras, and also that Warners expected total devotion for their wages. Reagan was hired at two hundred dollars a week, which grew to five hundred dollars over the next two years. By the start of filming *Kings Row* in 1941, he was earning one thousand dollars a week, which was not considered, even at that time, a startlingly good salary for a man who had been a well-known screen figure for four years. However, it was certainly a nice way to make a living and Reagan enjoyed a fine, albeit modest, lifestyle. He indulged in sports such as swimming, riding and golf, and avoided involvement in any scandalous or abnormal activities. He was not noted for being difficult with his employers or untoward in his social behavior. He enjoyed his good fortune and felt that he was a lucky man.

Ronald Reagan had known Jane Wyman since he joined Warners in 1937. She had been put under contract to the studio in 1936, but it was not until they were cast together in *Brother Rat* in the summer of 1938 that they became seriously interested in one another. Shortly after the completion of the film, they announced their engagement. Wyman made it known that her appetite for nightclubbing had diminished in favor of Reagan's love for sports, particularly football games. After a courtship of just over a year, and much comment about them being the ideal American couple, they were married on January 26, 1940. Louella Parsons had been the first to announce their engagement and had also taken them along on promotional tours. She gave them a wedding reception at her home.

At the time of their marriage, the Reagans were film players of about equal rank. They both earned about five hundred dollars a week, which enabled them to live a comfortable life but not one of star magnitude, although neither professed any great desire for a glittering lifestyle. Wyman's career continued on the level of a secondary player but Reagan's gradually increased in star status. She claimed considerable pride in this and backed him in his interests. In 1941 they appeared together in a short picture called *How to Improve Your Golf.*

On one occasion, Jane Wyman surprised her fans by announcing that marrying Reagan had changed her personality for the better. She claimed to have previously been an anxious and rather suspicious woman, and that he had helped her to become more

The star of a wartime flight training picture.

19

at ease with people. "He was such a sunny person. I never felt free to talk to anyone until I met Ronnie." Their happiness was increased with the arrival of a daughter, Maureen Elizabeth, on January 27, 1941, which was also Wyman's twenty-seventh birthday. The Reagans adopted a boy in 1945 whom they named Michael Edward. On June 26, 1947, another daughter was born to them, but the child was four months premature and died the following day.

Ronald Reagan qualifies as a family man. He claims to have enjoyed his youth in Illinois, despite the hard times, and both his marriages have been traditional domestic relationships. Shortly after his arrival in Hollywood, he brought his parents to live in Los Angeles, which also became the home of his brother Neil, who made a career in the advertising industry. By the time of the move to California, Jack Reagan's heart condition had worsened to the point where he could no longer work, but his actor son gave him the job of handling his fan mail.

Reagan's first four years in the movies were the enjoyable basis for a pleasant lifestyle, but contained few performances that offered dramatic satisfaction. It was not a career which could be listed as important in the film industry. He made an impact with his role as George Gipp in *Knute Rockne —All American*, but mostly Reagan portrayed a pleasing B hero or a solid supporting player to Warners' major stars. In 1941, Warners gave him a lead in *Kings Row*, a somber drama built along epic lines. His performance as a small-town playboy brought down by grim circumstances put him into the big film league. His agent, Lew Wasserman, tripled Reagan's salary, bringing him more than three thousand dollars a week. It was the lucky break for which all actors yearn, but it came at a time when it could do him little good. On April 14, 1942, Ronald Reagan was inducted into the United States Army.

Because of his commission in the cavalry reserve, Reagan was made a second lieutenant in that branch of the service, but because of his eyesight (he had discarded glasses for contact lenses) he was disqualified from combat duty. Reagan reported at Fort Dixon, San Francisco, and became a liaison officer in charge of loading transports. After a few dull months at Fort Dixon, Reagan was transferred to the rapidly expanding Army Air Corps. Reagan was then sent to the Hal Roach Studios, under Army jurisdiction during the war. The studio was located in Culver City, only ten miles from Warner Bros., enabling Reagan to live at home. The Roach studio soon acquired the Hollywood title of "Fort Wacky" because of the vast amount of movie talent in uniform stationed there, and also because of the actor's unconventional way of soldiering. It was less formal than most military posts, but most productive. "We would turn out training films and documentaries, and conduct a training school for combat camera units. All of the newsreel material in the theatres of bombings and strafings was the product of these units."

Reagan's years in the army were interrupted a number of times to permit him to appear in Hollywood's contributions to the war. He was relieved from duty for several weeks to make Warners' *This Is the Army*, a film which raised millions of dollars for service charities. Aside from his regular duties as a narrator and director of training films, he also appeared in the USO promotional film *Mr. Gardenia Jones* (1942), in which he played a lonely soldier in a strange town; *Rear Gunner* (1943), playing a downed pilot; and *For God and Country* (1944), a film about army chaplains, with Reagan as a Catholic priest. He also made appearances at events organized to support the war effort.

Reagan received his discharge from the army on December 9, 1945, by which time he held the rank of captain. He decided to enjoy a few months of vacation before returning to Warners and resuming his contract. Like many other stars making comebacks to the screen, it was not easy to enter the swing of things. New stars had appeared in the meantime, tastes had changed, and, indeed, the world itself had changed. Warners finally found a vehicle which they considered right for Reagan's re-entry into the movie world, *Stallion Road*, but they did not release it until March of 1947. By that time, Reagan had been off the screen for a long while. It was the first of twenty-two postwar movies he would be in before retiring from pictures. None of the films were ever another *Kings Row*. His salary was star status, resuming at thirty-five hundred dollars and increasing with the years, but it was not simply a matter of money. The films Reagan was making were not of sufficient value to increase his standing as a box office draw. With the making of *Hellcats of the Navy* in 1957, ten years after his return to the screen, his career was virtually over. But the Hollywood political scene was taking up more of Reagan's time, particularly the running of unions and guilds.

No matter how much Jane Wyman attempted to

In 1946 broadcaster Ted Malone visits the Reagans in their home to do a radio interview. Daughter Maureen was then five and son Michael was sixteen months.

share Reagan's interests, she was not enthusiastic about his growing involvement in politics. Wyman was often heard to remark, "He's very political— I'm not." By 1947, their marriage had lost its spark, and they drifted in different directions, he toward political matters and she toward film stardom. They formally separated in January of 1948, at which time Reagan spoke to the press of his continuing love for the somewhat strange lady who was his wife. He allowed that the death of their second daughter had been a tremendous strain on her, and that she had also been under stress with her long and difficult portrayal of *Johnny Belinda.* He added, "Perhaps, too, my seriousness about public affairs has bored Jane."

The rift between the Reagans was alluded to in 1973 when Father Robert Perrella published his book *They Call Me the Show Business Priest.* Father Perrella had been a friend of Wyman and wrote, "She admits it was exasperating to awake in the middle of the night, prepare for work, and have someone at the breakfast table, newspaper in hand, expounding on the far right, far left, the conservative right, the conservative left, the middle-of-the-roader. She harbors no ill feeling toward him."

Jane Wyman filed for divorce at the beginning of May, 1948, and was granted an interlocutory decree at the end of June. She received her final papers in July of the following year, giving her custody of the two children, a division of their properties and child support. Neither Reagan nor Wyman was involved

in gossip, and neither party was romantically linked with any other. Louella Parsons lamented that it was the saddest break-up of a seemingly ideal couple since Douglas Fairbanks and Mary Pickford. Reagan quipped, with some bitterness, that the only corespondent he could name in his ailing marriage was *Johnny Belinda.*

It is difficult to understand if Ronald Reagan's career suffered because of his passionate involvement in film industry politics. It is certain that he thus alienated many people who might have helped his career. His growing disenchantment with the kind of films in which he appeared must have been a factor. The making of only two or three movies a year left him with plenty of time for other pursuits. His interest in sports was constant and his love of horses and ranch life increased greatly.

Postwar Hollywood was a chaos, as studios tried to hold their audiences. Few felt sure of what to offer as movie entertainment. It was a much harsher world after the war, and the fluff of pre-war Hollywood films was out of favor. Unknown by the pub-

Reagan, the president of the Screen Actors Guild, confers with board director Edward Arnold in August of 1947, at a meeting to settle an industry conflict between two unions.

Reagan the horseman—and a very good one—taking one of his mounts around the track of his California ranch in 1948.

lic was the bitter, chaotic working side of Hollywood life. In their heyday, the studios treated workers with disdain in the matters of hours and wages. It was supposed to be fun to make movies, and an honor to be involved, while the moguls and their shareholders earned vast profits. The resultant union demands for labor laws were proportionately severe. During the war, the American Federation of Labor gave the country a no-strike pledge for the duration. The one place where that pledge was not honored was Hollywood. Toward the end of the war years, strikes rippled through the film industry. They were mostly moves to bring larger salaries and gain better working conditions, but there was evidence of larger political aspects, including talk of Communist take-over. People began polarizing their positions toward the Left and the Right.

This was the atmosphere in which Reagan returned to the picture business. He had long been an officer of the Screen Actors Guild and had joined the board in 1938, exhibiting a talent for bargaining and negotiating. Eventually he became a "rabid union man." After the war, his involvement grew even wider, and he joined many causes in his belief that the industry and the country were in trouble. Reagan looks back on those years at himself as a liberal of an almost extreme "bleeding heart" stripe. Aside from SAG, he served on the boards of the American Veterans Committee, and the Hollywood Independent Citizens Committee of Arts, Sciences and Professions. He also inadvertently found himself involved in organizations with increasingly leftist sympathies. While maintaining a set of liberal convictions, he began to campaign against Communist influence. He was joined by many famous Hollywood figures, but many people in Hollywood disagreed with these views. In October of 1947, Reagan was a witness before the House Committee on Un-American Activities in its investigation of Communism in the film industry. That same year, he was elected President of the Screen Actors Guild. In 1949 he was elected chairman of the Motion Picture Industry Council, representing labor, management and other factions. By that time his skills as an arbitrator were much respected.

In 1950 Ronald Reagan enjoyed a return to Dixon, Illinois, where he was honored for a week as a local boy who had made good. Not long after, he appeared on his first television show, an episode of CBS' "Airflyte Theatre," unaware at that time how important the medium would later become in his career. Over the next few years, he appeared in a dozen top television dramatic presentations, and in 1954, Reagan accepted an offer to become the host of "The General Electric Theatre." This may be regarded as one of the most important decisions in Reagan's life. It was not simply a matter of being the host and, occasionally, an actor on a series which ran eight years, but the opportunity helped to develop his skills as a lecturer and speechmaker. Part of his job was to work with the GE Public Relations Department to promote a company image, which included touring the United States and making personal appearances at GE's one hundred and thirty-five plants. He addressed the employees and their families on company policy, the role of

With the second Mrs. Ronald Reagan (Nancy Davis) on their honeymoon in 1952.

On the set of "Prisoner of War" (1954) Dewey Martin shows Nancy Davis and Reagan a coat worn by Paul Muni in "The Good Earth."

business in national life and the dangers of over-government. It is thought by many who know Reagan that his political nature emerged from his role as a GE lecturer. It was, of course, abetted by his involvement in Hollywood union politics. He resigned as president of SAG in 1952, but served on the board of directors until he was again elected president in 1959. In his second term as president, Reagan settled a strike which resulted in increased income and medical benefits for the members, but he resigned a year later when he felt his involvement in a production company would run counter to his union position.

Another major change in Reagan's life occurred on March 4, 1952, when he married actress Nancy Davis. They had met two years prior when Reagan was asked to help clear her of charges of communist leanings. It evolved that there was another woman of the same name in the film industry. During his efforts to help clear up this matter, Reagan discovered a lady who shared his views on politics and supported him in every way. Two years of courting culminated in a wedding in which Reagan's friend William Holden was the best man. The marriage has been described by all who know the couple as ideal, as well as one which further encouraged the actor's political abilities. Nancy Davis was the daughter of Dr. Loyal Davis, a distinguished neurosurgeon and a prominent political conservative. Reagan and his father-in-law no doubt found much in common politically and that the doctor was stimulating to his interests.

The host of "The General Electric Theater" (1954-1962), a greatly successful series and perhaps the most important level in Reagan's career as an actor.

If Reagan ever felt that he had not been a great Hollywood success before the war and that his postwar movie career was less than he had hoped for, his life after both his marriage and the appointment as a General Electric star spokesman brought him success on a more agreeable level. His income was satisfying, as was his field of work. He also enjoyed the pleasure of creating a second family when, on October 22, 1952, Patricia Ann Reagan was born in an emergency Caesarean operation. On May 20, 1958, Ronald Prescott Reagan arrived, also by Caesarean delivery. In 1954, the Reagans lived in a beautiful home in Pacific Palisades, about a mile from the ocean, and fortune seemed kind to a man who had begun life on the modest side of the tracks.

When the "General Electric Theatre" series

ended, Reagan was out of a job, but not for long. He was hired as the host of the veteran television series "Death Valley Days," with its entertaining brief yarns about life in western America. It was a pleasant assignment for Reagan, who occasionally played the lead in the stories, but his days as an actor were drawing to a close.

Ronald Reagan finally traded in his Democratic Party membership for the Republican cause in 1962. He had been a Democrat for Eisenhower and a Democrat for Nixon, but throughout the fifties, his political sentiments veered more and more to the Right. By the early sixties he was an active campaigner against Communism, and in 1964 supported both Barry Goldwater for president and George Murphy in the California senatorial election. A speech he made that year on behalf of Goldwater

Reagan became the host of another veteran television series in 1964—"Death Valley Days." At times he played the lead, as in this episode, "A City Is Born," which told the story of Arizona land developer Charles Poston.

reportedly drew more contributions than any other in political history. These efforts did not go without notice, and in 1965 a group of California businessmen formed a group called The Friends of Ronald Reagan, to support him in running for the office of governor of California.

On November 8, 1966, Ronald Reagan was elected governor with a 57.8 percent of the vote, giving him more than eight hundred thousand votes over Edmund G. Brown. Reagan served two terms and his supporters claim that during those eight years he reduced government spending and rebated millions of dollars to taxpayers. For Californians, the most indelible memory of the Reagan administration was his tough attitude toward the state's academic troubles. He won much admiration for his refusal to tolerate student strikes and demands at the taxpayer's expense.

After the completion of his term as governor, Reagan returned to his Pacific Palisades home and devoted his time to writing newspaper columns on political matters and to preparing a daily five-minute broadcast. In the Gallup Poll of January, 1975, he was given ninth place among the most admired Americans. By the end of the year, Reagan had decided to enter the contest for the presidency of the United States, but his campaigning met with

At a testimonial dinner for Jack L. Warner in 1973, the guest speaker was an ex-Warner employee, then the governor of California. Warner looks as if he can hardly believe it.

defeat at the Kansas City Republican convention in August of 1976. His party had picked Gerald Ford to contest Jimmy Carter—and lost. Political pundits now speculate over what might have happened had the Republicans chosen Reagan instead of Ford.

In 1980, the Republicans selected Ronald Reagan as their candidate for President. The result . . . as the bartender in the musical comedy *Irma la Douce* says, "that's another story," and another book. This one is about an actor and his films.

On "The Dean Martin Comedy Hour" (NBC, September 14, 1973), Martin guides a roast of the California governor.

THE FILMS

LOVE IS ON THE AIR

A Warner Bros. First National Picture,
Directed by Nick Grinde,
Produced by Bryan Foy,
Written by Morton Grant, based on a story by Roy
** Chanslor,**
Photographed by James Van Trees,
Running time: 61 minutes.

CAST:
Andy McLeod (Ronald Reagan); *Dunk Glover* (Eddie Acuff); *J. D. Harrington* (Robert Barrat); *Weston* (Raymond Hatton); *Les Quimby* (Willard Parker); *Pinkie* (Spec O'Donnell); *Mouse* (Tommy Bupp); *Lang* (Jack Mower); *Jo Hopkins* (June Travis); *Nicey Ferguson* (Ben Weldon); *E. E.*

With June Travis.

With William Hopper.

With Robert Barrat.

Nichols (Addison Richards); *Bill* (Dickie Jones); *Eddie Gould* (William Hopper); *Mr. Copelin* (Herbert Rawlinson); *Mr. Butler* (Harry Hayden); *Mrs. Copelin* (Mary Hart).

Love Is on the Air has nothing to do with love actually being broadcast. Audiences in October of 1937 might well have expected this modest programmer to be a musical, since Dick Powell's *Varsity Show,* released the previous month, contained him singing "Love Is on the Air, Tonight," of which he had also made a Decca recording. What the audiences got was a minor crime picture, with twenty-six-year-old Ronald Reagan making his movie debut as a crusading radio announcer. Since his profession prior to becoming an actor was being an actual radio announcer, he could hardly have made an easier transition into a new medium.

Reagan's debut film was shot in a three-week schedule and was a rehash of the 1934 Paul Muni picture *Hi, Nellie,* the vague title of which no doubt

helped make it one of that fine actor's least memorable screen vehicles. It offered Muni a chance to delve into lighter, more comedic material than the drama with which he was until then associated. Muni's role was that of a free-wheeling newspaper editor who is demoted to the lovelorn column for embarrassing his employers with his attempts to flush out gangsters. But those attempts soon become successful and bring a promotion.

The Reagan version is set in a smalltown radio station and finds him being demoted to children's programming when his sponsors complain to the station manager (Robert Barrat) about Reagan's assertions regarding local crime. The demotion does nothing to dampen the young announcer's resolve to uncover the connections between racketeers, local businessmen and the politicians who provide protection for profit. The kiddie show host (June Travis) whose job he usurps is at first resentful, but it is not long before she takes his side in romance as well as the crusade. It then transpires that the department store sponsor (Addison Richards) who complained about the announcer's insinuations is himself linked with the racketeers. When the head of the Better Business Bureau is murdered, the announcer redoubles his efforts to expose local crime. He becomes a hero when he tricks the racketeers into revealing themselves before an open microphone.

With Eddie Acuff.

With Eddie Acuff.

With Cliff Saum, June Travis and Eddie Acuff.

33

With Robert Barrat and June Travis.

Love Is on the Air, playing as second feature on Warner double billed programs, accomplished what it was intended to do, which was to provide passable entertainment and to introduce a new actor. Like most B films, it did not receive major reviews, but the trade magazines referred to Reagan as "likeable" and "pleasing," and *Variety* pointed out that the actor was at his best when engaged in fast physical action.

It may not have been a brilliant start to a movie career but it was a solid one which gave Reagan cause to feel optimistic and gave Warners a reason to feel they had added a good player to their team.

HOLLYWOOD HOTEL

A Warner Bros. First National Picture,
Directed by Busby Berkeley,
Produced by Hal B. Wallis,
Written by Jerry Wald, Maurice Leo and Richard
   Macauley,
Photographed by Charles Rosher and George
   Barnes,
Songs by Johnny Mercer and Richard W. Whiting,
Music direction by Leo F. Forbstein,
Running time: 103 minutes.

CAST:
Ronnie Bowers (Dick Powell); *Virginia* (Rosemary Lane); *Mona Marshall* (Lola Lane); *Fuzzy* (Ted Healy); *Georgia* (Johnnie Davis); *Alexander Dupre* (Alan Mowbray); *Alice* (Frances Langford); *Louella Parsons* (Herself); *Chester Marshall* (Hugh Herbert); *Jonesy* (Glenda Farrell); *Ken Nyles* (Himself); *Bernie Walden* (Allyn Joslyn); *Callaghan* (Edgar Kennedy); *Dress Designer* (Curt Bois); *Cameraman* (Eddie Acuff); *Dot Marshall* (Mabel

With Lola Lane, Dick Powell, Ted Healy, Allyn Joslyn, Hugh Herbert and Rosemary Lane.

Todd); *Jerry Cooper* (Himself); Benny Goodman and His Orchestra; Raymond Paige and His Orchestra.

Ronald Reagan may have been somewhat surprised at the methods of his employers with this second assignment. He had just played the lead in a film, albeit a B; yet they next slotted him into the finale of *Hollywood Hotel* and then neglected to give him a screen credit. The bit in *Hollywood Hotel* gave him experience in what was Warners' last impressive musical of the thirties. The cycle had begun with *42nd Street* five years earlier and flourished in high style with the cinematic choreography of Busby Berkeley and talents like Dick Powell, Ruby Keeler and Joan Blondell. The profusion of lavish production numbers diminished as America emerged from the Great Depression and moviegoers no longer needed so much the fanciful escapism of the Berkeley surrealism. *Hollywood Hotel,* directed entirely by Berkeley, contains none of the splendiferous routines for which he had become famous. Instead it relies more on comedy, characters, and a large selection of songs and band numbers.

Hollywood Hotel was a natural outgrowth of the radio series of that name which premiered on the CBS Radio Network October 5th, 1934. Sponsored by Campbell's Soups, it was the first major Hollywood network production and paved the way for the establishment of the film capital as America's foremost point for live radio programming. The host was Dick Powell, whose popularity in the movies was enlarged by his radio career. The driving force behind the program was the powerful gossip columnist Louella Parsons, whose movie industry clout allowed her to populate the show with a copious selection of Hollywood talent.

The film is not a celluloid version of the radio show, but instead has Powell, a saxophone player with Benny Goodman's band, winning a talent contest trip to Hollywood. Little but frustration comes of his foray into the movie world, but with the help of his girl friend (Rosemary Lane), he eventually snares an appearance on Louella's stellar radio show, and enjoys immediate success.

Reagan appears at the scene of the broadcast as one of Louella's staff, presumably an announcer. He looks pleased, although a trifle stiff, no doubt because he was just out of smalltime radio and suddenly found himself amidst a glittering array of the biggest of Big Time Radio personalities.

With Louella Parsons.

SWING YOUR LADY

A Warner Bros. Picture,
Directed by Ray Enright,
Associate Producer: Samuel Bischoff,
Written by Joseph Schrank and Maurice Leo, based
   on the play by Kenyon Nicholson and Charles
   Robinson,
Photographed by Arthur Edeson,

Music by Adolph Deutsch,
Songs by M. K. Jerome and Jack Scholl,
Running time: 79 minutes.

CAST:
Ed Hatch (Humphrey Bogart); *Popeye Bronson*
(Frank McHugh); *Sadie Horn* (Louise Fazenda);

With Humphrey Bogart.

Joe Skopapoulos (Nat Pendleton); *Cookie Shannon* (Penny Singleton); *Shiner Ward* (Allen Jenkins); *Waldo Davis* (Leon Weaver); *Ollie Davis* (Frank Weaver); *Mrs. Davis* (Elvira Weaver); *Jack Miller* (Ronald Reagan); *Noah Webster* (Daniel Boone Savage); *Smith* (Hugh O'Connell); *Rufe Horn* (Tommy Bupp); *Len Horn* (Sonny Bupp); *Mattie Horn* (Joan Howard); *Mabel* (Sue Morris); *Hotel Proprietor* (Olin Howland); Speciality Number (Sammy White).

Humphrey Bogart rarely spoke of his early Warner films, but he is known to have considered *Swing Your Lady* to be among the worst. Ronald Reagan learned with this assignment that not all films could easily be identified as either an A or a B product but that there was a degree between the two categories. The picture might be billed as a main feature, but it was usually relegated to being shown at theatres in the first part of the week rather than the weekends. There wasn't much Reagan could learn from his brief role in *Swing Your Lady*—it required no more of him than to portray a glib-tongued sports reporter and was simply another brief assignment in his breaking-in process at Warners.

Bogart, undoubtedly seething with indignation over the casting, appears as a slick promoter down on his luck and stranded in a small Kentucky town. His main asset is a dim hulk of a wrestler (Nat Pendleton). The promoter is impressed with the virility of a lady blacksmith (Louise Fazenda) and hatches the idea of matching her with his wrestler, but the wrestler falls in love with the lady and refuses to fight. The promoter's dilemma is solved when the lady's hillbilly suitor returns to town and objects to the proposed match. A match between the wrestler and the suitor is arranged, with the winner to marry the Amazonian blacksmith. The wrestler is the victor, but he deserts the promoter in favor of smalltown life.

Swing Your Lady is amusing, but too far-fetched to make any real comedic impact. Scattered throughout its seventy-nine minutes are five songs by M. K. Jerome and Jack Scholl. They help the pacing but fail to stay in the memory. One is titled "Dig Me a Grave in Missouri," and could reflect Bogart's feelings after viewing himself in this film.

With Louise Fazenda, Penny Singleton and Humphrey Bogart.

SERGEANT MURPHY

A Warner Bros. Picture,
Directed by B. Reeves Eason,
Produced by Bryan Foy,
Written by William Jacobs, based on a story by Sy
   Bartlett,
Photographed by Ted McCord,
Running time: 57 minutes.

CAST:
Private Dennis Murphy (Ronald Reagan); *Mary Lou Carruthers* (Mary Maguire); *Colonel Carruthers* (Donald Crisp); *Corporal Kane* (Ben Hendricks); *Major Gruff* (William Davidson); *Sergeant Connors* (Max Hoffman, Jr.); *Lieutenant Duncan* (David Newell); *Major Smythe* (Emmett Vogan); *Texas*

With Mary Maguire.

39

With Max Hoffman, Jr.

(Tracy Lane); *Adjudant* (Edmund Cobb); *Joan* (Ellen Clancy); *Alice* (Rosella Towne); *Bess* (Helen Valkis); *Henry* (Sam McDaniels).

After several bit parts in A pictures, Ronald Reagan was happy to be reassigned to Bryan Foy's B unit and return to a lead role. *Sergeant Murphy* had been bought by Warners as an A vehicle for James Cagney, but the shrewd star turned it down after reading the script. No matter how charming the material, it was a minor yarn, although Reagan welcomed the chance to act in a story about horses that allowed him to use his knowledge of the United States Cavalry, in which he was a reserve officer.

Bryan Foy wisely chose for his director B. Reeves Eason (1886-1956), a man with a special talent for filming horses in action. Eason had staged the chariot race in *Ben Hur* (1926) and had also directed the incredible finale of *The Charge of the Light Brigade* (1936). *Sergeant Murphy* contained nothing on the epic scale, but it did require a direc-

tor with the knack of filming horse training and horse races.

The title of the film refers to a horse. Reagan plays a cavalry private who is devoted to the horse, an animal with a gift for jumping, but with ears so sensitive that the sound of artillery makes him skittish and unreliable for army duties. The soldier spares the horse heavy duties, trains him and later gains possession of him. He is aided by the daughter (Mary Maguire) of the post colonel (Donald Crisp), a connection which evolves into love for both the private and the horse. Once the horse is mustered out of the army, the trio undergoes a variety of experiences, some near tragic, and eventually the horse wins acclaim in national shows. Sergeant Murphy is smuggled into England and entered in the Grand National.

Based on a true story, *Sergeant Murphy* is a fine example of a lost art—the making of well-crafted B pictures. It affords an interesting view of 1938 army life and cavalry training. The racing sequences are

40

With Mary Maguire.

With Mary Maguire.

expertly staged by Eason, with the Santa Anita Racetrack doubling for the famed British course.

For Reagan, making the film was enjoyable because much of the footage was filmed on locations. He recalls, "We drove up the beautiful Monterey Peninsula, to the 11th Cavalry, where all the outdoor shooting would take place. This was a little more homelike and familiar to me than the sound stage at the studio. Playing a cavalryman, surrounded by regular army personnel, was reminiscent of my last few years at Fort Des Moines."

With Mary Maguire and Sergeant Murphy.

With Mary Maguire and Donald Crisp.

With Donald Crisp, Sam McDaniel and Mary Maguire.

ACCIDENTS WILL HAPPEN

A Warner Bros. Picture,
Directed by William Clemens,
Produced by Bryan Foy,
Written by George Bricker and Anthony Coldeway,
Photographed by L. William O'Connell,
Running time: 62 minutes.

CAST:

Eric Gregg (Ronald Reagan); *Patricia Carmody* (Gloria Blondell); *Jim Faber* (Dick Purcell); *Nora Gregg* (Sheila Bromley); *Blair Thurston* (Addison Richards); *John Oldham* (Hugh O'Connell); *Mary Tarlton* (Janet Shaw); *Burley Thorne* (Elliott Sulli-

With Gloria Blondell.

Hugh O'Connell, Gloria Blondell, Dick Purcell and Addison Richards.

With Burley Thorne, Hugh O'Connell, Addison Richards, Dick Purcell and Gloria Blondell.

van); *Dawson* (Anderson Lawlor); *Space* (Spec O'Donnell); *Nudnick* (Kenneth Harlan); *Dorsey* (Don Barclay); *Doctor Faris* (Earl Dwire); *Doc* (Max Hoffman, Jr.); *Cosgrove* (John Butler).

Nothing cinematic that Ronald Reagan had yet done at Warners strained him as an actor. His film image as a "likeable," "breezy," and "good natured" fellow was forming. But with *Accidents Will Happen*, Reagan was required to deepen his image with several character problems. While nothing more than a modest B picture, the theme grappled with substantial material—the growing manipulation of insurance companies by fraudulent claims. It was a practice prevalent by 1938, and the picture drew its subject matter from actual newspaper reports of such crimes. B pictures often dealt with workaday America more honestly than the glossy A films. Alistair Cooke stated that, as a young reporter, he gained a more realistic view of American life from minor films than from more splendid Hollywood productions.

With Elliott Sullivan.

In *Accidents Will Happen,* Reagan plays a naive insurance adjustor married to a girl (Sheila Bromley) with a taste for material pleasures which he can ill afford. Her ethics are far less than his and she chisels his accounts. Not only does he lose his job, but his wife testifies against him and joins forces with the gang under investigation. The husband's despair is lightened by the love of a cigar stand girl (Gloria Blondell, sister of Joan). They become slick operators of the phony claim business, and when they have gained enough evidence, they call in the police to nab the crooks. The young man gets back his job and resumes his career as an adjuster, plus a new life with the right girl.

With Allan Cavan.

With Gloria Blondell and Sheila Bromley.

With Sheila Bromley.

COWBOY FROM BROOKLYN

A Warner Bros. Picture,
Directed by Lloyd Bacon,
Produced by Lou Edelman,
Written by Earl Baldwin, based on the play *Howdy, Stranger* by Louis Peletier, Jr., and Robert Sloane,

Photographed by Arthur Edeson,
Songs by Richard Whiting, Johnny Mercer and Harry Warren,
Running time: 77 minutes.

With Pat O'Brien.

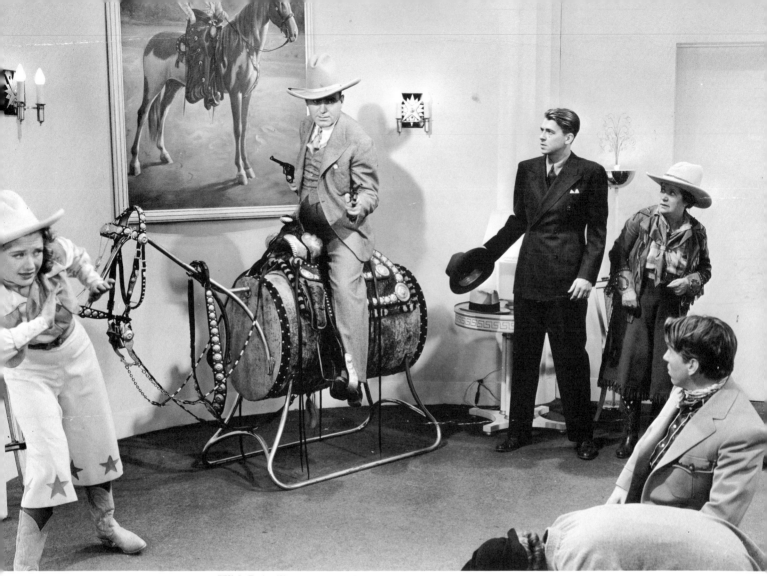

With Priscilla Lane, Pat O'Brien, Emma Dunn and Johnnie Davis.

CAST:

Elly Jordan (Dick Powell); *Roy Chadwick* (Pat O'Brien); *Jane Hardy* (Priscilla Lane); *Sam Thorne* (Dick Foran); *Maxine Chadwick* (Ann Sheridan); *Jeff Hardy* (Johnny Davis); *Pat Dunn* (Ronald Reagan); *Ma Hardy* (Emma Dunn); *Pop Hardy* (Granville Bates); *Professor Landis* (James Stephenson); *Mr. Jordan* (Hobart Cavanaugh); *Mrs. Jordan* (Elisabeth Risdon); *Abby Pitts* (Dennie Moore); *Panthea* (Rosella Towne); *Mrs. Krinkenheim* (May Boley); *Louie* (Harry Barris); *Spec* (Candy Candido).

With the Warners cycle of lavish musicals at an end, the studio had difficulty finding vehicles for their major musical star, Dick Powell. Powell was not displeased over the ending of the musicals, since he believed (and later proved) that his talents were more than being merely a light baritone. He had been badgering Warners for better material and could have considered *Cowboy From Brooklyn* as a step in the right direction. Although the script might have seemed like a likely comedy, on celluloid the story was only mildly amusing and did nothing to help Powell's career.

The cowboy of the title is played by Powell, although he is actually a city dude with a great fear of animals—even chickens and gophers. Horses terrify him. As the story begins he is a drifter who gets thrown off a train while traveling through the west. He stumbles upon a dude ranch, whose owners take pity on him and offer a job when they discover he has a nice singing voice. He does well as a host, provided he stays away from the livestock. A slick show-biz promoter (O'Brien) and his associate (Reagan) arrive, both down on their luck. After hearing Powell sing, the promoter decides to make him into a radio singing cowboy. The scheme works and the dude becomes a favorite of the airwaves, which is fine until he is expected to make personal appearances at events like rodeos. The daughter (Priscilla Lane) of the rancher helps him with hypnosis, and while in a trance he performs bravely, but he occasionally slips out of the state and reveals his cowardice. He eventually succeeds at performing as a cowboy hero at Madison Square Garden, thanks largely to the loving support of his western girlfriend.

Cowboy From Brooklyn approaches being a satire of the singing cowboys who were in such a vogue during the thirties, particularly the phony publicity surrounding them. The film fails because of the ridiculous character Powell plays, but his songs were good, and one of the numbers, "Ride, Tenderfoot, Ride," survives as a perennial western ballad.

The film was a welcome opportunity for Ronald Reagan to work with Powell and O'Brien, who both made Reagan feel welcome, but who did not alert him to what he was doing wrong in his characterization. In order not to be swamped by O'Brien's fast talking Broadway hustler, Reagan was playing his character as a drawling slow talker. His lines kept being cut, yet as a newcomer to film making, he was too nervous to ask the director why. One of the character players finally took him aside and explained that his drawling delivery was killing the scenes and forcing O'Brien to speak even faster. Once that embarrassing point had been made, Reagan turned to O'Brien for advice on how best to

With Dick Powell, Pat O'Brien, Hobart Cavanaugh and Elisabeth Risdon.

With Hobart Cavanaugh and Dick Powell.

play his lines.

Reagan recalls, "The very next scene called for me to make an entrance in Grand Central Station, face a battery of the press, and, complete with straw hat and cane, do a carnival shill act introducing our cowboy discovery. Bacon must really have been dying, figuring how he would rewrite this scene to get rid of slowpoke me." But Reagan had grown wise to what was needed, and when the director yelled for action, he came onto the set like a true hustler, bouncing his cane off the floor and launching into his pitch. "There were no more rewrites."

52

BOY MEETS GIRL

A Warner Bros. Picture,
Directed by Lloyd Bacon,
Produced by George Abbott,
Written by Sam and Bella Spewack,
Photographed by Sol Polito,
Music direction by Leo F. Forbstein,
Running time: 90 minutes.

CAST:
Robert Law (James Cagney); *J. C. Benson* (Pat O'Brien); *Susie* (Marie Wilson); *C. Elliott Friday* (Ralph Bellamy); *Rossetti* (Frank McHugh); *Larry Toms* (Dick Foran); *Rodney Bevan* (Bruce Lester); *Announcer* (Ronald Reagan); *Happy* (Paul Clark); *Peggy* (Penny Singleton); *Miss Crews* (Dennie

when Warners bought the property, they had Olsen and Johnson in mind for the leads. The insanely antic pair were unable to clear their commitments in order to do the film, and Warners offered it to Cagney, who had just returned to the studio after a two year absence. Cagney accepted the offer, provided that Lloyd Bacon was assigned as director rather than George Abbott, who had directed the play and was being considered for the film. Cagney also insisted on his chum Pat O'Brien as costar. O'Brien, Cagney and Bacon had made so many films together that they were a performing team. The results are clearly evident in *Boy Meets Girl*, which moves right along.

The film is set in Warners' studio at Burbank and affords film buffs interesting shots of picture-making activity of the day. The tone is one of wild spoof, with Cagney and O'Brien as a pair of writers badly in need of an immediate idea for a picture. Their studio supervisor (Ralph Bellamy) has lost patience with them, but is constantly being bamboozled when he tries to get rid of them. The studio's cowboy star (Dick Foran) needs a good picture to save his sagging career and the writers devise a typical boy-meets-girl story. They invent a part for the infant son of a studio waitress (Marie Wilson) and build the role until the cowboy star becomes insecure. The project reaches the screen and becomes a triumph for the studio—and the baby.

Boy Meets Girl was a fair success due mostly to Cagney's popularity, but audiences needed to know a great deal more about the motion picture industry to appreciate its full sting. It is a wonder that the film was made at all in view of its searing satire of studio functioning, particularly the questionable intelligence and judgment of producers.

Ronald Reagan is the eager young radio announcer who comments on the elaborate movie premiere at the Carthay Circle Theatre, the Los Angeles theatre which was used many times in movies about Hollywood. His glib spiel is in keeping with the frantic pace of *Boy Meets Girl,* and he was no doubt aware of the inside joke of this particular scene. The year prior to this, Warners had bought a screenplay from Errol Flynn called *The White Rajah*. It was never made into a movie because they didn't consider it good enough, despite Flynn's badgering. The film being given its premiere at the Carthay Circle Theatre, with young Reagan welcoming the guests, was Errol Flynn in *The White Rajah!*

Moore); *Songwriters* (Harry Seymour and Bert Hanlon); *Major Thompson* (James Stephenson); *B. K.* (Pierre Watkin); *Cutter* (John Ridgely); *Office Boy* (George Hickman); *Smitty* (Cliff Saum); *Commissary Cashier* (Carole Landis); *Dance Director* (Curt Bois).

Up to this point in Reagan's Hollywood career, the fledgling actor's appearances in Warners products had not utilized his potential acting talents. *Boy Meets Girl* joined these ranks to again require him to play a radio announcer in the last reel. The most important aspect of the film for Reagan was contact with its stars, James Cagney and Pat O'Brien, who became—and still are—close friends. Reagan's Irish blood qualified him for membership in the Emerald Isle clan at Warners.

Boy Meets Girl is one of Hollywood's better self-examinations, possibly because it was written by Broadwayites Sam and Bella Spewack. It was generally assumed that the models for the pair of wacky screenwriters who are the protagonists of the story were the wonderfully talented but wild Charles MacArthur and Ben Hecht. *Boy Meets Girl* had been a success as a Broadway play, with Jerome Cowan and Allyn Joslyn as the writers, and

GIRLS ON PROBATION

A Warner Bros. Picture,
Directed by William McGann,
Produced by Bryan Foy,
Written by Crane Wilbur,
Photographed by Arthur Todd,
Running time: 63 minutes.

CAST:
Connie Heath (Jane Bryan); *Neil Dillon* (Ronald Reagan); *Tony Rand* (Anthony Averill); *Hilda Engstrom* (Sheila Bromley); *Judge* (Henry O'Neill); *Kate Heath* (Elisabeth Risdon); *Roger Heath* (Sig Rumann); *Jane Lennox* (Dorothy Peterson); *Mrs.*

With Jane Bryan.

With Sig Rumann, Elisabeth Risdon and Jane Bryan.

With Susan Hayward, Joseph Crehan and Jane Bryan.

Engstrom (Esther Dale); *Gloria Adams* (Susan Hayward); *Terry Mason* (Larry Williams); *Mr. Engstrom* (Arthur Hoyt); *Ruth* (Peggy Shannon); *Marge* (Lenita Lane); *Prison Inmate* (Janet Shaw); *Dave Warren* (James Nolan); *Todd* (Joseph Crehan); *Prosecuting Attorney* (Pierre Watkin); *Public Defender Craven* (James Spottswood); *Head Matron* (Brenda Fowler).

The title of this pedestrian programmer is misleading, since it deals with a young woman and her problems with the law. Connie (Jane Bryan) is a nice, innocent girl. Her troubles start when a guest (Susan Hayward) at a party accuses her of stealing the evening gown she is wearing, causing her to be arrested. The gown had been loaned by a friend, Hilda (Sheila Bromley), who works with Connie in a dry cleaning shop. The guest withdraws her

charge, but the insurance company covering the shop decides to prosecute, and Connie is tried for grand larceny. A bright, young attorney (Reagan) believes her story and manages to get her off with a suspended sentence, but her father (Sig Rumann) is far less understanding and orders her to leave home.

Connie gets a job in another city, where she runs into her wayward friend Hilda, who is involved in a bank robbery with her racketeer lover (Anthony Averill). During the crime, Connie gets pushed into the getaway car. When the robbers are caught by the police, she is tried as an accomplice and given a probated sentence of three years. She returns to her hometown and takes a job with the young attorney, but does not tell him of her current trouble with the law. Connie and her employer fall in love and plan their marriage, but Hilda reappears and threatens Connie with exposure and blackmail. Connie coop-

With Elisabeth Risdon, Sig Rumann and Jane Bryan.

erates with the police and the racketeer is brought to justice. The racketeer fights to the death with Hilda. Connie is rewarded for her honesty in the arms of her attorney lover.

Even if it had been made with more flair, *Girls on Probation* would have been nothing more than a passable B flick. But with its limp direction and a dull script, the film quickly sank into obscurity. The only interesting point for film buffs is the casting of

Susan Hayward in her first substantial role as a Warners starlet. Like Reagan, she had appeared in the finale of *Hollywood Hotel* (as a guest sitting at a table), but her association with Warners was not a happy one. Her later film career did not develop until she joined Paramount in 1939. Hayward and Reagan were part of a Warners promotional tour in 1938 and seem not to have found anything much in common with each other.

BROTHER RAT

A Warner Bros. Picture,
Directed by William Keighley,
Produced by Robert Lord,
Written by Richard Macaulay and Jerry Wald, based
on the play by John Monks, Jr., and Fred F.
Finkelhoffe,

Photographed by Ernest Haller,
Running time: 90 minutes.

CAST:
Billy Randolph (Wayne Morris); *Joyce Winfree*
(Priscilla Lane); *Bing Edwards* (Eddie Albert); *Dan*

With Wayne Morris and Eddie Albert.

With Eddie Albert, Wayne Morris and Johnnie Davis.

With Gordon Oliver, Johnnie Davis and Wayne Morris.

Crawford (Ronald Reagan); *Claire Adams* (Jane Wyman); *Kate Rice* (Jane Bryan); *A. Furman Townsend, Jr.* (Johnny Davis); *Colonel Ramm* (Henry O'Neill); *Mistol Bottom* (William Tracy); *Harley Harrington* (Larry Williams); *Captain Rogers* (Gordon Oliver); *Mrs. Brooks* (Jessie Busley); *Jenny* (Louise Beavers); *Tripod Andrews* (Robert Scott); *Newsreel Scott* (Fred Hamilton); *Coach* (Oscar Hendrion); *Nurse* (Isabel Jewell).

Eddie Albert, after several years as a New York stage and radio actor, made his breakthrough to fame with his performance in George Abbott's 1937 Broadway production of the comedy *Brother Rat.* When Warners bought the screen rights, they used Albert, but had writers Richard Macaulay and Jerry Wald demote his character from the lead to only a supporting role. In the film version, Wayne Morris plays the lead, with Ronald Reagan rounding out

the group in this amusing tale of three military cadets. In spite of his reduced status, Eddie Albert stole the picture and triggered a long Hollywood career for himself.

The story is set at the Virginia Military Institute, often called the West Point of the South. The title refers to the fond pet name cadets had for each other. In the last few weeks before graduation, the wild-spirited trio attempt to get themselves in shape in order to pass muster. Billy (Morris) is the wildest boy, but Dan (Reagan) runs a close second as they break most of the academy rules, particularly those about staying up after hours and leaving the grounds to visit their girlfriends. Bing (Albert) has a more disturbing problem—he is secretly married, although it is forbidden, and he receives news that his bride is pregnant. Bing is nearly reduced to a nervous wreck, but his chums do their best to cover for him. Since they are also engaged in a variety of

With Eddie Albert and Jane Wyman.

With Wayne Morris, William Tracy and Johnnie Davis.

pranks on and off campus, their best is often inadequate. The daring Dan makes his academy life even more dangerous by romancing the commandant's daughter (Jane Wyman). Things get very sticky when the pregnant bride (Jane Bryan) appears for the end-of-term football game and prom. Hiding the girl in the barracks is only one of the many comic complications. All of the cadets win their sheepskins, but only after the most confusing circumstances have been worked out.

Brother Rat gives a good account of life at VMI and speaks well for academic-military life, despite the pranksters' antics. The film did well for Warners and advanced Reagan's career by revealing his flair for light comedy. Says Reagan, "There is room for only one discovery in a picture. Eddie Albert stole the honors, and deservedly so." There was a more personal discovery for Reagan while working on *Brother Rat*—it was his first screen assignment with Jane Wyman, out of which developed their romance and marriage.

62

With Wayne Morris and Eddie Albert.

With Wayne Morris, Jane Wyman, Priscilla Lane and Eddie Albert.

With Jane Wyman, Priscilla Lane and Wayne Morris.

GOING PLACES

A Warner Bros. Cosmopolitan Picture,
Directed by Ray Enright,
Produced by Hal B. Wallis,
Written by Jerry Wald, Sig Herzig and Maurice Leo,
   based on the play *The Hottentot* by Victor Mapes
   and William Collier, Sr.
Photographed by Arthur L. Todd,
Songs by Johnny Mercer and Harry Warren,
Running time: 84 minutes.

CAST:
Peter Mason (Dick Powell); *Ellen Parker* (Anita Louise); *Droopy* (Allen Jenkins); *Jack Withering* (Ronald Reagan); *Franklin Dexter* (Walter Catlett); *Maxie* (Harold Huber); *Frank* (Larry Williams); *Colonel Withering* (Thurston Hall); *Cora Withering* (Minna Gombell); *Joan* (Joyce Compton); *Frome* (Robert Warrick).

With Anita Louise, Janet Shaw, Dick Powell, Minna Gombell, Rosella Towne and Larry Williams.

With Minna Gombell and Anita Louise.

Warners got plenty of mileage out of the play *The Hottentot,* by William Collier, Sr., and Victor Mapes. They did it first in 1923 with Douglas Mac-Lean, and again in 1929 as a talkie with Edward Everett Horton. In 1936 it was the basis for Joe E. Brown's *Polo Joe.* Two years later, the studio decided to dust it off again as a vehicle in which to star Dick Powell. The only memorable thing about this version is that it produced the great song, "Jeepers Creepers," even though not sung by Powell. The script called for the song to be sung to a horse called Jeepers Creepers and the performer was the horse's groom, played by Louis Armstrong.

The thin plot calls for Powell to act as a sporting goods salesman posing as a famous gentleman jockey in order to infiltrate the home of a wealthy Maryland horseman, Colonel Withering (Thurston Hall). His pleasing personality enables him to become a member of the wealthy horsey set, including the colonel's dashing son (Reagan) and his lovely niece (Anita Louise). His success becomes a problem when he falls in love with the niece, since he is then expected to ride the colonel's horses, and, of course, he doesn't know how to ride. He manages to perform well during a ride by a fluke, which leads to him being chosen to perform in a race with the

colonel's prize horse, Jeepers Creepers. The horse is one of wild temperament and can be pacified only when it hears its song sung by its groom. The groom becomes indispensable to the phony gentleman's hopes of not being revealed. The race is won by having the groom and his musician friends ride in a truck along the racetrack and lead Jeepers Creepers to victory.

Going Places is a fond memory for Ronald Reagan because of his growing friendship with Dick Powell and the luxury of being paid to work with horses. Attired in natty riding garb, Reagan looks happy in a breeze of a role. The film called for extensive shooting at a ranch, renowned for its stock training, and for polo sequences filmed at the Will Rogers State Park. Rogers had been a polo enthusiast and had laid out magnificent grounds for the sport. It was a favorite gathering spot in the thirties for Hollywood's horsey set, which included Ronald Reagan.

With Larry Williams, Thurston Hall, Anita Louise and Minna Gombell.

With Robert Warwick, Minna Gombell, Dick Powell, Thurston Hall, Anita Louise and Walter Catlett.

SECRET SERVICE OF THE AIR

A Warner Bros. Picture,
Directed by Noel Smith,
Produced by Bryan Foy,
Written by Raymond Schrock, based on material
compiled by W. H. Moran,
Photographed by Ted McCord,
Running time: 61 minutes.

CAST:

Lieutenant Brass Bancroft (Ronald Reagan); Saxby (John Litel); Pamela Schuyler (Ila Rhodes); Jim Cameron (James Stephenson); Gabby Watters (Eddie Foy, Jr.); Zelma Warren (Rosella Towne); Dick Wayne (Larry Williams); Joe LeRoy (John Ridgely); Hefer (Anthony Averill); Hamrick (Bernard Nedell); Doc (Frank M. Thomas).

With Rosella Towne.

With Bernard Nedell.

With John Litel.

Due to his increased popularity from *Brother Rat,* Warners starred Ronald Reagan in a series of adventure films. The studio had acquired the memoirs of William H. Moran, a former chief of the United States Secret Service and Bryan Foy was assigned to use the material. He decided it was good for Reagan, but as the actor recalls, "I'm sure the Secret Service wasn't exciting enough for Brynie, and he threw away everything but the title. I became the Errol Flynn of the B's. I was as brave as Errol, but in a low-budget fashion."

The hero of *Secret Service of the Air* is "Brass" Bancroft, a former army air corps lieutenant who makes a living as a commercial pilot, until he joins the Secret Service. Why the character gives up a comfortable job for one of danger is not made clear,

but once in the government's employ, Brass plunges into his assignments with courage and energy. His first job is to uncover the villains operating an airborne smuggling ring bringing aliens into the United States, and to do this he poses as a counterfeit money agent.

For this initial picture in the series, Warners gave *Secret Service of the Air* higher than usual production values, especially in Ted McCord's fine aerial photography, and in the employment of stuntmen. Producer Foy gave his brother Eddie, Jr., the continuing role of Bancroft's genial sidekick Gabby. John Litel, one of Warners' busiest stock character actors, got the role of Saxby, Bancroft's boss, and the villain is suavely played by the dapper James Stephenson. The most jarring sequence in the picture is one in which a plane load of aliens are dropped into the air when the floor of the passenger compartment opens up because the smugglers fear they are about to be apprehended. In the climax, the hero grapples with the villain in the cockpit of a plunging plane as the villain tries to open the plane's hatch door.

The film did well as the second feature of weekend bills, particularly on Saturday afternoons when it was paraded before youngsters as the main fea-ture. Reagan, for a while, joined the ranks of junior matinee idols like Flash Gordon and the Lone Ranger. Since he was still young and in good physical shape because of his sports activities, Reagan did his own on-film fighting. The budget allowed for a double for the villain, but not for the hero; thus many of the fight sequences were shot over the villain's shoulder, centering on the hero's efforts. Reagan recalls that it was often painful and that he sustained several black eyes during his adventures as Brass Bancroft.

With Eddie Foy, Jr.

With Larry Williams and Eddie Foy, Jr.

**With producer Bryan Foy and W. H. Moran, the
former head of the United States Secret Service, on whose files the series with Reagan was based.**

DARK VICTORY

A Warner Bros. First National Picture,
Directed by Edmund Goulding,
Produced by Hal B. Wallis,
Associate Producer: David Lewis,
Written by Casey Robinson, based on the play by
  George Emerson Brewer, Jr., and Bertram Bloch,
Photographed by Ernest Haller,
Music by Max Steiner,
Running Time: 106 minutes.

CAST:

Judith Traherne (Bette Davis); *Dr. Frederick Steele* (George Brent); *Michael O'Leary* (Humphrey Bogart); *Ann King* (Geraldine Fitzgerald); *Alec Hamm* (Ronald Reagan); *Doctor Parsons* (Henry Travers); *Carrie Spottswood* (Cora Witherspoon); *Miss Wainwright* (Dorothy Peterson); *Martha* (Virginia Brissac); *Colonel Mantle* (Charles Richman); *Doctor Carter* (Herbert Rawlinson); *Doctor Driscoll*

With Bette Davis.

With Geraldine Fitzgerald and Bette Davis.

Around Reagan: Cora Witherspoon, John Ridgely and Bette Davis. Bartender: Sidney Bracy.

(Leonard Mudie); *Miss Dodd* (Fay Helm); *Lucy* (Lottie Williams).

Dark Victory is so much a Bette Davis picture that it is difficult to remember the other stars. George Brent comes to mind only when one film buff asks another, "Who played the husband?" Geraldine Fitzgerald is easier to recall, due to the warmth of her "best friend" portrayal. But the fact that Humphrey Bogart had a key role in *Dark Victory* surprises more than Bogart admirers. As for Ronald Reagan's role in the film, his fifth billing could as easily be fifteenth. The role would have been hard for any actor to make important, but Reagan's lack of rapport with director Edmund Goulding makes it a portrayal that he does not care to dwell on. Nevertheless, it is the most prestigious film in which he had appeared during his career at that point.

The film is simply a highly crafted soap opera, and one that any film detective can easily spot as a prime Warners product of its time. The style, pacing, editing, the fine black-and-white photography of Ernest Haller, who did so many of the best Davis pictures and the romantic, pulsating score by Max Steiner are all ingredients that make for a distinct brand of tear-jerker. Bette Davis says of Steiner, who wrote the music for nineteen of her pictures, "He knew more about drama than any of us."

Bette Davis' portrayal of the lead character, Judith Traherne, is one of the most memorable in her screen history. Judith is a wealthy Long Island socialite given to a giddy lifestyle. Confident of her affluence and her power over men, she is unprepared for tragedy, which strikes in the form of a brain tumor. The underlying honesty and courage with which she faces this affliction eventually prove her to be a woman of substance. Among her friends is Ann King (Fitzgerald), her secretary, and dashing young Alex Hamm (Reagan), who steer her toward brain specialist Dr. Frederick Steele (Brent). The doctor diagnoses her malady as one which will end her life within a year. Judith falls in love with him and accepts his proposal of marriage. When she discovers that her tumor is fatal, she assumes the doctor's proposal is born of pity, and rejects it, returning to the social whirl. The one serious concern in her life is her thoroughbred horse, whose trainer (Bogart) candidly points out her false pride.

74

With Bette Davis and Geraldine Fitzgerald.

Judith realizes she has a chance for happiness and marries the doctor. They enjoy an idyllic few months together, but in time her sight begins to fail. When her husband leaves to attend a medical conference, she feigns good health. Her last hours are spent alone, and she is comforted by the feeling that she has achieved some measure of victory over the darkness dealt to her.

Reagan's role in *Dark Victory* is that of a rich, frequently inebriated young blade of Judith Traherne's social set, who loves her but fails to make any real impression. Edmund Goulding, a veteran with a reputation for directing with taste and elegant style, saw Reagan's role as more epicene than the actor did, in that the young man would not be macho enough to win a woman like Judith. Reagan felt he could not accommodate himself to this view; however, he tried and afterwards regretted it. "We came to our moment of truth near the end of the

picture. In the scene George Brent comes to my apartment, desperate because of his failure to convince Bette that he loves her. She, in turn, thinks his love is pity because they both know she is dying. My part in the scene is to tell George she is on her way to the apartment, and before I disappear I ask him to be kind to her because I love her too. It was a well-written scene, and a nice moment in the picture. I still insist there is only one way to play a scene and that is simply and with great sincerity. Our director hit the ceiling. He demanded, 'Do you think you are playing the leading man? George has that part, you know.' In the matter of studio standing, I was outweighed. He was a top director, doing only top pictures. I was up in that class on a raincheck. He didn't get what he wanted, whatever the hell that was, and I ended up not delivering the line the way my instinct told me it should be delivered. It was bad."

CODE OF THE SECRET SERVICE

A Warner Bros. Picture,
Directed by Noel Smith,
Produced by Bryan Foy,
Written by Lee Katz and Dean Franklin,
Photographed by Ted McCord,
Running time: 58 minutes.

CAST:
Lt. Brass Bancroft (Ronald Reagan); *Elaine* (Rosella Towne); *Gabby Watters* (Eddie Foy, Jr.); *Friar Parker* (Moroni Olsen); *Ross* (Edgar Edwards); *Decker* (Jack Mower); *Crackett* (John Gallaudet); *Saxby* (Joe King); *Butch* (Steven Darrell); *Dutch* (Sol Gorss).

With Eddie Foy, Jr., and Paul Panzer.

With Rosella Towne and Edgar Edwards.

For his second time out as Brass Bancroft of the Secret Service, Ronald Reagan was sent into a remote part of Mexico to discover the operations of a band of American counterfeiters. After plates are stolen from the United States Mint, Brass traces them to a mountain hideaway but gets snared by the thieves. They pin the blame on him for the death of a fellow agent, and Brass is slated for execution. He breaks out of his Mexican jail but again falls into the hands of the counterfeiters, along with the daughter (Rosella Towne) of an American rancher. The pair are seemingly doomed to be blown up, along with the counterfeiting evidence, but Brass overpowers a guard and escapes, taking the young lady with him. He then lures the smooth leader (Moroni Olsen) of the counterfeiters back across the United States border and there arrests him.

Code of the Secret Service provided a scant hour's worth of entertainment for Saturday matinee audiences. The reviewer for *Variety* commented that it was the kind of far-fetched stuff that Pearl White used to suffer through. Reagan's own attitude was tongue-in-cheek. He walked on the set and asked director Noel Smith, "When do I fight, and whom?" Smith stated a time and pointed out the opponent.

After *Code* was completed, producer Bryan Foy took on the job of shaping it into an acceptable movie. Foy had the reputation at Warners of being able to edit almost any length of celluloid into something worth projecting. This one was bad, and he backed Reagan when the actor appealed to the studio to not release it. Warners compromised and released it everywhere except the Los Angeles-district, thereby enabling Reagan to escape embarrassment among his friends. Reagan later visited a distant city and noticed the title on a marquee. As he stood outside the theatre looking at the posters of stills, he realized that the ticket taker had recognized him when he said, "You should be ashamed."

NAUGHTY BUT NICE

A Warner Bros. Picture,
Directed by Ray Enright,
Written by Jerry Wald and Richard Macaulay,
Photographed by Arthur L. Todd,
Songs by Johnny Mercer and Harry Warren,
Running time: 90 minutes.

CAST:

Professor Hardwick (Dick Powell); *Linda McKay* (Gale Page); *Zelda Manion* (Ann Sheridan); *Aunt Martha* (Helen Broderick); *Joe Dirk* (Allen Jenkins); *Aunt Penelope* (Zasu Pitts); *Ed Clark* (Ronald Reagan); *Killer* (Maxie Rosenbloom); *Allie Gray*

With William Davidson, Dick Powell, Gale Page, Helen Broderick, Zasu Pitts, Vera Lewis and Elizabeth Dunne.

With Dick Powell, Helen Broderick, Gale Page, Allen Jenkins and Jerry Colonna.

(Jerry Colonna); *Aunt Annabella* (Vera Lewis); *Aunt Henriette* (Elizabeth Dunne); *Stanislau Pysinski* (Luis Alberni); *Sam Hudson* (Bill Davidson); *Judge* (Granville Bates); *Dean Burton* (Halliwell Hobbes); *Band Leader* (Peter Lind Hayes).

Naughty but Nice brought the Warner Bros. phase of Dick Powell's long career to a rather tepid end. The original title of this minor musical was *The Professor Steps Out*, which indicates the general plot of the story. By the summer of 1938, Powell was anxious to exit his Warner contract. He had joined the studio seven years before, and had appeared in twenty-seven Warner musicals. Some were classics, but after 1937, there was a swift decline in quality. *Naughty but Nice* was not any improvement, and the studio delayed its release until June of 1939, by which time Powell had left Warner

Bros. Ann Sheridan's stock was climbing, so she was given top billing. For Ronald Reagan, it was simply one more small part in his dizzying round of studio chores in 1938.

The professor in *Naughty but Nice* is a naive smalltowner who tackles New York with the purpose of getting his symphonic composition published. He is badly equipped to meet the kind of sharks who manipulate music in Tin Pan Alley. Part of his problem is that he has been coddled by three maiden aunts who believe him to be a genius. The professor's music is not entirely without merit, and in fact has enough melodic content to be bowdlerized into pop material. His main work is filched and turns up as a jive song called "Hooray for Spinach," performed by a slinky singer (Ann Sheridan).

The singer vamps the composer for her own purposes, but a lovely lady lyricist (Gale Page) also falls in love with him. Another character who is on the professor's side is an honest music publisher (Reagan). *Naughty but Nice* is mildly amusing, mostly when it satirizes pop music merchants lifting material from the classics, but the joke grows stale in this mediocre screenplay.

Reagan says about Dick Powell, who had made him welcome at the studio and always given him encouragement, "I was one of the thousands who were drawn to this very kind man, and who would think of him as a best friend. Sometimes our paths took us in different directions, and months would pass without our seeing each other. Still in these later years, when we did meet again, it would be as if no interruption had occurred. I cannot recall Dick ever saying an unkind word about anyone."

With Gale Page, Dick Powell, Helen Broderick and Stuart Holmes.

HELL'S KITCHEN

A Warner Bros. Picture,
Directed by Lewis Seiler and E. A. Dupont,
Produced by Mark Hellinger and Bryan Foy,
Written by Crane Wilbur and Fred Niblo, Jr.,
Photographed by Charles Rosher,
Running time: 81 minutes.

CAST:
Tony (Billy Halop); *Joey* (Bobby Jordan); *Gyp* (Leo Gorcey); *Ace* (Huntz Hall); *Bingo* (Gabriel Dell); *Ouch* (Bernard Punsley); *Soap* (Frankie Burke); *Beth* (Margaret Lindsay); *Jim* (Ronald Reagan); *Buck* (Stanley Fields); *Crispin* (Grant Mitchell);

With Margaret Lindsay.

82

Steve Garvy (Frederic Tozere); *Jed Crispin* (Arthur Loft); *Sarah Crispin* (Vera Lewis); *Hardy* (Robert Homans); *Flugue* (Charles Foy); *Callahan* (Robert Strange); *Whitey* (Raymond Bailey); *Mr. Quill* (Clem Bevans); *Judge Chandler* (George Irving).

Ronald Reagan's assignment to *Hell's Kitchen* could almost be taken literally. It was a Dead End Kids picture and the real-life loud manners and prankishness of the young actors who made up the team of screen delinquents had caused other actors to refuse to work with them. Says Reagan, "It was an experience similar to going over Niagara Falls the hard way—upstream. Counting noses and getting them all in one scene was a major chore, but sometimes it was a relief when they did take off and disappear for a few hours. You never knew when a canvas chair would go up in smoke or be blown apart by the giant firecrackers they were never without. Having heard lurid tales from other actors, I approached my first picture with them in something of a sweat."

Reagan's concern about working with the Dead End Kids was solved by a conversation with James

With Gabriel Dell and Leo Gorcey.

With Stanley Fields.

With Stanley Fields, Margaret Lindsay and Charles Foy.

With Stanley Fields, Margaret Lindsay, and the Dead End Kids.

With Stanley Fields, Charles Foy, Frankie Burke and Huntz Hall.

With Grant Mitchell, Stanley Fields and Ila Rhodes.

Cagney, who had not only worked with them, but had been a product of the same New York area which had spawned the Kids. Cagney advised Reagan, ''Just tell them you look forward to working with them but you'll slap hell out of them if they do one thing out of line.'' The advice was effective.

Hell's Kitchen finds the kids having graduated from reform school and assigned to a ''Boy's Town'' type of city shelter. The shelter is run by a cruel and crooked superintendent (Grant Mitchell), who is assisted by an ex-racketeer (Stanley Fields) on probation. This rough, tough character enjoys trying to straighten out the kids and joins with them in getting the superintendent kicked out of his job. Also on hand in trying to run the shelter along correct lines are two social workers (Reagan and Margaret Lindsay), whose tentative romance is railroaded into the real thing through the cupidic efforts of the kids.

The street-wise cinematic touch of New Yorker Mark Hellinger is apparent in the picture. He produced it under the supervision of Bryan Foy, but the script wavers in balancing earthy humor and social comment. Part of the trouble stems from the film having two directors—Lewis Seiler and E. A. Dupont. Possibly Seiler found the Dead End Kids hard to handle. *Hell's Kitchen* is, in any case, one of the less successful of the Warner social crusade pictures.

85

ANGELS WASH THEIR FACES

A Warner Bros. Picture,
Directed by Ray Enright,
Produced by Robert Fellows,
Written by Michael Fessier, Niven Busch and Robert
 Buckner, based on an idea by Jonathan Finn,
Photographed by Arthur L. Todd,
Music by Adolph Deutsch,
Running time: 76 minutes.

Cast:
Joy Ryan (Ann Sheridan); *Pat Remsen* (Ronald Reagan); *Billy Shafter* (Billy Halop); *Peggy Finnegan* (Bonita Granville); *Gabe Ryan* (Frankie Thomas); *Bernie* (Bobby Jordan); *Sleepy Arkelian* (Bernard Punsley); *Lee Finnegan* (Leo Gorcey); *Huntz* (Huntz Hall); *Luigi* (Gabriel Dell); *Mr. Remsen* (Henry O'Neill); *Martino* (Eduardo Ciannelli);

With Ann Sheridan.

Mayor Dooley (Berton Churchill); *Maloney* (Minor Watson); *Miss Hannaberry* (Margaret Hamilton); *Alfred Goonplatz* (Jackie Searle); *Kroner* (Bernard Nedell); *Hynos* (Cy Kendall); *Shuffle* (Dick Rich); *Gildersleeve* (Grady Sutton); *Turnkey* (Aldrich Bowker); *Mrs. Arkelian* (Marjorie Main).

James Cagney had scored a great hit in 1938 playing a meanhearted gangster in *Angels With Dirty Faces*, in which he was featured with the Dead End Kids. *Angels Wash Their Faces* was more of a follow-up than a sequel and did not match the impact of the Cagney picture. Ronald Reagan and Ann Sheridan got top billing, but in parts that were lackluster compared to the Cagney material. The film is purely a Dead End Kids outing.

With Ann Sheridan.

With Ann Sheridan and Frankie Thomas.

When one of the gang, Gabe Ryan (Frankie Thomas), is framed as an arsonist and indicted by an insurance company, his chums, who call themselves The Termites, determine to clear him. They become model citizens and cooperate with a stalwart district attorney (Henry O'Neill) and his son (Reagan), who is in love with Gabe's sister (Ann Sheridan). One of the gang (Billy Halop) becomes mayor during Boy's Week, and appoints his friends to various civic posts on his staff. They gather the evidence that enables the district attorney and his son to nab the real arsonists. Gabe is cleared, and with the loud vocal support of The Termites, the sister and the district attorney's son march to the altar.

Ronald Reagan thus survived a second film with the Dead End Kids, and fortunately for his career, he was not asked to work with them again.

With Minor Watson, Bill Halop, Gabriel Dell, Bobby Jordan and Frankie Thomas.

With Leo Gorcey, Bill Halop, Ann Sheridan, Bobby Jordan, Frankie Thomas, Gabriel Dell and Bonita Granville.

With Ann Sheridan and Cy Kendall.

SMASHING THE MONEY RING

A Warner Bros. Picture,
Directed by Terry Morse,
Produced by Bryan Foy,
Written by Anthony Coldeway and Raymond
  Schrock,
Photographed by James Van Trees,
Running time: 57 minutes.

CAST:
Lieutenant Brass Bancroft (Ronald Reagan); *Peggy* (Margot Stevenson); *Gabby Watters* (Eddie Foy, Jr.); *Dice Matthews* (Joe Downing); *Parker* (Charles D. Brown); *Danny* (Elliott Sullivan); *Gordon* (Don Douglas); *Milrane* (Charles Wilson); *Saxby* (Joe King); *Warden* (William Davidson); *Guard Davis*

With Eddie Foy, Jr.

With Eddie Foy, Jr., and Joe King.

(Dick Rich); *Guard Sheldon* (Max Hoffman, Jr.); *Night Captain* (John Hamilton).

The third Secret Service adventure yarn in Ronald Reagan's catalog deals, like the second, with counterfeiting, but with somewhat more credibility. Brass Bancroft and his sidekick Gabby (Eddie Foy, Jr.) are assigned to track a gang of phony moneymakers, who have flooded the country with bad bills. Following up on a tip from the underworld, Brass pretends to be a counterfeiter and has himself thrown into prison. He there discovers that the gang is printing the bogus bills on the premises, on the

With Elliott Sullivan, John Hamilton and Joe Downing.

prison press. After engineering a jail break, Brass leads his government colleagues to the source of the operation.

The title, *Smashing the Money Ring*, told audiences what to expect of this film, and if they didn't expect more, they could be satisfied. It was a typical crime story and, according to Reagan, much script doctoring was done during the shooting. The more glaring dramatic holes were plugged, but as with all small budgets and tight schedules, the B product left the studio with only a kiss and a promise from producers and actors.

90

With Margot Stevenson, Eddie Foy, Jr., and William Davidson.

With Dick Rich.

With Dick Rich, William Davidson, John Hamilton and Eddie Foy, Jr.

BROTHER RAT AND A BABY

A Warner Bros. Picture,
Directed by Ray Enright,
Produced by Robert Lord,
Written by Jerry Wald and Richard Macaulay, based
on a story by Fred F. Finkelhoffe and John Monks, Jr.,
Photographed by Charles Rosher,
Music by Heinz Roemheld,
Running time: 87 minutes.

With Jane Wyman.

With Jane Wyman and Priscilla Lane.

CAST:
Billy Randolph (Wayne Morris); *Joyce Winfree* (Priscilla Lane); *Bing Edwards* (Eddie Albert); *Dan Crawford* (Ronald Reagan); *Claire* (Jane Wyman); *Kate* (Jane Bryan); *"Commencement"* (Peter B. Good); *Harley Harrington* (Larry Williams); *McGregor* (Arthur Treacher); *Colonel* (Moroni Olsen); *Mrs. Brooks* (Jessie Busley); *Sterling Randolph* (Paul Harvey); *Mr. Harper* (Berton Churchill); *Mrs. Harper* (Nana Bryant); *Girl in Bus* (Mayo Methot); *Cab Driver* (Ed Gargan).

The popularity of *Brother Rat* called for a sequel, but the result was a considerable disappointment to the public. The same team of writers were employed to concoct a follow-up to the antics of the three Virginia Military Institute graduates (Wayne Morris, Eddie Albert and Ronald Reagan). The boyish escapades that seemed amusing in uniform became merely childish and silly in civilian clothes. In this offering, Reagan spends most of his time continuing his courtship of the daughter (Jane Wyman) of the VMI Commandant (Moroni Olsen) and incurring his wrath by keeping her out until dawn.

The central device of the sequel is the campaign of his buddies to get Bing (Albert) a job as sports coach at VMI. They fail to do this, and so persuade Bing and his wife (Jane Bryan), with their baby (Peter B. Good), to come to New York. The wild ideas of Billy (Morris) get them in trouble, and in one of his many moments of desperation over lack of money, he steals a violin and pawns it. The improbable adventures somehow work out, and Billy plants the baby on an airplane bound for a goodwill tour of Peru. The resultant publicity gets Bing the job at VMI, Dan (Reagan) wins his girl and Billy winds up in the arms of a lovely southerner (Priscilla Lane).

Brother Rat and a Baby, a minor item on Hollywood's list of screwball comedies, quickly sank from sight.

With Wayne Morris, Priscilla Lane and Jane Wyman.

With Paul Harvey and Wayne Morris.

93

With Priscilla Lane, Wayne Morris, Eddie Albert and Jane Bryan.

With Priscilla Lane, Wayne Morris, Jane Bryan,
Eddie Albert, Peter B. Good and Jane Wyman.

AN ANGEL FROM TEXAS

A Warner Bros. Picture,
Directed by Ray Enright,
Produced by Robert Fellows,
Written by Fred Niblo, Jr., and Bertram Millhauser,
    based on the play *The Butter and Egg Man* by
    George S. Kaufman,
Photographed by Arthur L. Todd,
Music by Howard Jackson,
Running time: 69 minutes.

CAST:
Peter Coleman (Eddie Albert); *Mr. McClure* (Wayne Morris); *Lydia Weston* (Rosemary Lane); *Marge Allen* (Jane Wyman); *Mr. Allen* (Ronald Reagan); *Valerie Blayne* (Ruth Terry); *Quigley* (John Litel); *Mr. Robelink* (Hobart Cavanaugh); *Addie Lou Coleman* (Ann Shoemaker); *Chopper* (Tom Kennedy); *Peach Davis* (Milburn Stone); *Carvey* (Elliott Sullivan); *Louis* (Paul Phillips); *Bon-*

With Jane Wyman.

ham (Emmett Vogan); *Mayor O'Dempsy* (Ferris Taylor).

Warner Bros. cashed in on the marriage of their contract players Ronald Reagan and Jane Wyman by giving them the roles of husband and wife in *An Angel From Texas.* The studio was also still trying to work the popularity of the film *Brother Rat,* slotting Eddie Albert and Wayne Morris in the top spots in the cast listing.

Few dramatic vehicles have had as much film use as George S. Kaufman's 1925 Broadway comedy *The Butter and Egg Man.* The play was first transferred to the screen in 1928 by First National, a company that was soon thereafter purchased by Warners, who acquired the story rights. The studio used it as the basis for their 1932 Joe E. Brown picture, *The Tenderfoot,* and gave the script to their British division, who produced it as *Hello, Sweetheart* three years later. In 1937 it turned up as

With Eddie Albert and Wayne Morris.

With Wayne Morris, Rosemary Lane and Eddie Albert.

With Wayne Morris and Eddie Albert.

Dance, Charlie, Dance, with Stuart Erwin, and then in 1940 as *An Angel From Texas.* The play then became *Three Sailors and a Girl* in 1953, starring Jane Powell and Gordon MacRae. None of these films were major successes, and all used only the plot skeleton of Kaufman's play, that of an innocent man with money to invest who is persuaded to put it into a stage production. The "angel" in the 1940 title refers to the show business term for a financial backer.

The innocent in the Warner film is a nice young Texan (Eddie Albert) who sends his girlfriend (Rosemary Lane) off to New York where she hopes to become an actress. Instead, she becomes a secretary to a glib producer (Wayne Morris), and his more dignified partner (Reagan). The producers need backing for their new show, and as the innocent arrives in town with his mother's savings of

$20,000 with plans to invest it in a hotel, the producers fast-talk him into investing the money in their play. The innocent makes one condition—that his girlfriend must have the lead role. This presents a problem for the producers, who have committed the role to Valerie Blayne (Ruth Terry). She threatens them with a visit from her gangster friends if she doesn't get the part, but fortunately, she is a terrible actress, leaving the way open for the Texas girlfriend. The play, which was to be a heavy drama, is so silly when performed straight that it gets laughs and the show is turned into a successful farce.

An Angel From Texas was a rather amusing film, but it didn't do much to advance Reagan's career in the movies. By this point, he had made too many of these thin scripted films to be assigned any major roles.

97

MURDER IN THE AIR

A Warner Bros. Picture,
Directed by Lewis Seiler,
Produced by Bryan Foy,
Written by Raymond Schrock,
Photographed by Ted McCord,

Running time: 55 minutes.

CAST:
Brass Bancroft (Ronald Reagan); *Saxby* (John Litel); *Joe Garvey* (James Stephenson); *Gabby Waters*

(Eddie Foy, Jr.); *Hilda Ryker* (Lya Lys); *Doctor Finchley* (Robert Warrick); *Rumford* (Victor Zimmerman); *Admiral Winfield* (William Gould); *Commander Wayne* (Kenneth Harlan); *Jerry* (Frank Wilcox); *George Hayden* (Owen King); *John Kramer* (Dick Rich); *Otto* (Charles Brokaw); *Dolly* (Helen Lynd); *Prescott* (Jeffrey Sayre); *Sunnyvale* (Carlyle Moore, Jr.); *Police Chief* (Cliff Clark); *Congressman Rice* (Ed Stanley); *Captain Riddel* (Selmer Jackson); *Hargrave* (John Hamilton).

With Dick Rich (left).

The last of Ronald Reagan's Secret Service movies is also the best. At fifty-five minutes, it is the shortest of his feature films, but the trim adventure yarn was made more interesting with footage Bryan Foy had acquired of a dirigible crashing in the ocean. It was common practice in the making of B pictures to use stock footage, which in this case was the reason for scenarist Richard Schrock to write a story utilizing the exciting material.

Murder in the Air is a minor contribution to Hollywood's 1940 awareness of the growing wave of espionage in America. The film opens with a Washington investigating committee discussing the progress of foreign agents in this country. Brass Bancroft is assigned by his boss (John Litel) to bring into custody a suspected spy named Joe Garvey (James Stephenson), on whom the agency had been unable to gather evidence. When a well known spy is killed in a train wreck the death is covered and Bancroft assumes the dead man's identity. Our hero meets Garvey, who tells him to board the United States Navy dirigible Mason and examine a new device called "The Inertia Projector," a death ray that can bring down airplanes within a radius of four miles. Bancroft discovers that one of the officials on the ship is working for Garvey and is intent on stealing the blueprints of the invention. He saves the projector from destruction, but during a storm at sea, the enemy agent escapes with the machine's plans. Once safely back on land, Bancroft uses the projector to bring down the plane in which Garvey is making his escape.

With Cliff Clark and Eddie Foy, Jr.

Ronald Reagan, again in the guise of Brass Bancroft, for the last time, serves his country and saves it from the forces of evil. The junior league audiences would have watched further Bancroft adventures, but after three years as a utilitarian actor—a star of B movies and a bit player in A's—Warners gave Reagan's career an upward turn.

With Eddie Foy, Jr.

KNUTE ROCKNE— ALL AMERICAN

A Warner Bros. Picture,
Directed by Lloyd Bacon,
Produced by Hal B. Wallis,
Written by Robert Buckner, based on material
supplied by Mrs. Knute Rockne,
Photographed by Tony Gaudio,
Music by Ray Heindorf,
Running time: 98 minutes.

With Pat O'Brien.

Knute Rockne (Pat O'Brien); *Bonnie Rockne* (Gale Page); *George Gipp* (Ronald Reagan); *Father Callahan* (Donald Crisp); *Father Nieuwland* (Albert Basserman); *Chairman* (John Litel); *Doctor* (Henry O'Neill); *Gus Dorais* (Owen Davis, Jr.); *Lars Knutson Rockne* (John Qualen); *Martha Rockne* (Dorothy Tree); *Knute as a boy* (John Sheffield); *Harry Stuhldreher* (Nick Lukats); *Elmer Laydon* (Kane Richmond); *Don Miller* (William Marshall); *James Crowley* (William Byrne); *Reporter* (John Ridgely).

Aside from his role in *Kings Row*, the best remembered film of Ronald Reagan is his portrayal of football legend George Gipp in *Knute Rockne—All American*. It is also his personal favorite among the roles he has played, and one that he pursued with great determination. As a sports announcer at station WHO in Des Moines, Reagan once told his audiences about the renowned Gipp; about how he ran eighty yards through the Notre Dame's varsity the first time he put on a football uniform and how he went on to become one of the finest footballers of all time. Reagan had mentioned to producers at

With Pat O'Brien.

Warners that they should make a movie about the famed Notre Dame coach Knute Rockne, and that Pat O'Brien was ideal for the part, with Reagan as Gipp. The studio had no doubt about casting O'Brien, but the choice of Reagan was questioned. Ten other young actors were tested for the role and all were told, like Reagan, that they didn't look like football players. Reagan showed photographs of himself in uniform at college games, and explained that he had been able to attend college only because of his prowess at football. With that he was tested and given the part.

The Warner film is among the best made on the subject of football, as well as being a respectable treatment of the Rockne story. In preparing his screenplay, Robert Buckner used the files of the University of Notre Dame and the private papers of Rockne's widow, who was also present during the making of the film. Many of the football sequences were shot at Loyola University. The film follows Rockne's life from his childhood in Norway and his teenage years around Chicago, where he played sandlot football. Rockne as played by Pat O'Brien is seen working his way through Notre Dame as a postal clerk. He stays on to teach and to coach, and marries his sweetheart Bonnie Skiles (Gale Page).

The film shows the inception of the famous Rockne passing attack, devised with Gus Dorais (Owen Davis, Jr.), and of his tactical shift, as well as his relationship with George Gipp and the legendary Notre Dame Four Horsemen. The procession of gridiron victories is spoiled by Rockne's affliction with phlebitis, but the crippling illness does nothing to daunt his game spirit and his dedication to clean sportsmanship. His life comes to a premature end in a plane crash, and he is given a deeply moving funeral oration in the Notre Dame Chapel.

Knute Rockne—All American pays tribute to a gentleman of the sports world. In the opinion of Ronald Reagan, Pat O'Brien is a gentleman of the film world. When Reagan was tested for the part of Gipp, he fully expected, as is the usual procedure, to play his scene opposite a minor contract actor. Instead he came to the set and found O'Brien fully made up for his part and ready to play the crucial few minutes that would decide if Reagan got the job. The test scene was the one in which Gipp, ordered to carry the ball at his first practice, cocks an eyebrow and asks the coach, "How far?"

Reagan had not received much comment on his acting ability during his career. He was always considered to be a pleasing and competent player. With

With Gale Page.

the Rockne film he received compliments in every review, mostly that he was a perfect choice for the gifted but doomed football player. It was a role that occupied little more than one reel of the picture, but no actor could have asked for more. The part has an arresting entrance, a solid middle and a touching death scene, as the young man succumbs to pneumonia. On his death bed he tells Rockne, "Some day when things are tough, maybe you can ask the boys to go in there and win just once for the Gipper." At the end of the film, when the Notre Dame team seems on the verge of being defeated by the Army team, Rockne electrifies their sagging spirits by calling on them to "win one for the Gipper"— thereby giving Pat O'Brien the most famous line in his long career in films.

103

With Pat O'Brien.

Reagan's career moved ahead a giant step because of his work in this film. Having been almost a star for three years, he was now a name to reckon with. "It was the springboard that bounced me into a wider variety of parts in pictures. It's true, I got some unmerited criticism from sports writers. One of them wondered why producers never picked real football players for such parts. As I practically earned my way through college playing football, that disturbed me. However, this criticism was nicely balanced by some unmerited praise from the same general source, for another sports writer said I was so accurate in my portrayal of Gipp that I even imitated his slight limp. Actually, I wasn't trying to limp. I just wasn't used to my new football shoes and my feet hurt."

With Donald Crisp, Ruth Robinson and Pat O'Brien.

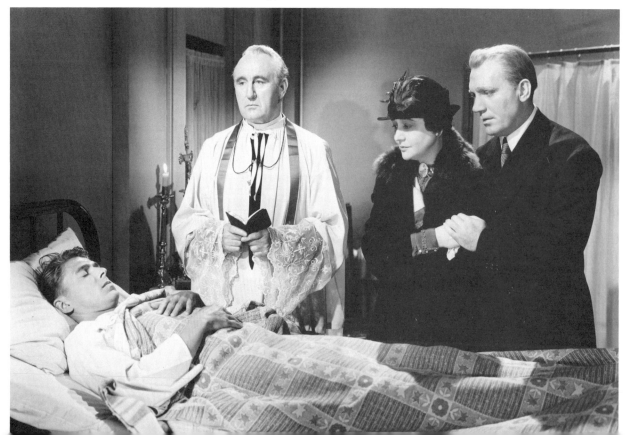

TUGBOAT ANNIE SAILS AGAIN

A Warner Bros. Picture,
Directed by Lewis Seiler,
Produced by Bryan Foy,

Written by Walter De Leon, based on the character
created by Norman Reilly Raine,
Photographed by Arthur Edeson,

With Marjorie Rambeau and Jane Wyman.

With Victor Killian, Paul Hurst, Marjorie Rambeau and Jane Wyman.

With Marjorie Rambeau, John Hamilton and Alan Hale.

With Marjorie Rambeau and Alan Hale.

Music by Adolph Deutsch,
Running time: 77 minutes.

CAST:

Tugboat Annie (Marjorie Rambeau); *Peggy Armstrong* (Jane Wyman); *Eddie King* (Ronald Reagan); *Captain Bullwinkle* (Alan Hale); *Alec Severn* (Charles Halton); *J. B. Armstrong* (Clarence Kolb); *Pete* (Paul Hurst); *Sam* (Victor Kilian); *Shiftless* (Chill Wills); *Captain Mahoney* (Harry Shannon); *Captain Broad* (John Hamilton); *Limey* (Sidney Bracy); *Johnson* (Jack Mower); *Rosie* (Margaret Hayes); *Miss Morgan* (Josephine Whittell); *Rex Olcott* (Neil Reagan); *Bradley* (George Meander).

Marie Dressler scored one of her biggest hits with her portrayal of *Tugboat Annie* (1933), the warm but grizzled old salt who captains a tugboat, and there would doubtlessly have been a sequel made if her death the following year had not intervened. MGM considered several actresses to take the role, but never selected one. In 1940, Warners acquired the rights to the Norman Reilly Raine characteriza-

tion and took a chance on Marjorie Rambeau, hoping that if the revival were successful, a series might be born. *Tugboat Annie Sails Again* did only mild business, however, and the idea of making a series was dropped. The critics commented that it was pointless to attempt to imitate Marie Dressler and that Miss Rambeau's version of the gruff, malapropistic old gal was good, but did not compete.

The part of Annie's husband, played in 1933 by Wallace Beery, was dropped and in the Warner version, she is a widow running a vessel called the *Narcissus* in the port of Secoma (presumably a combination of Seattle and Tacoma). Her chief competitor in the tugboat business is Captain Bullwinkle (Alan Hale), who heckles her at every opportunity. The company for whom Annie works needs a loan of $25,000, and she manages to get it for them. This brings her the job of towing a drydock to Alaska, but she is forced to hand it over to another captain. She goes along for the ride and saves the situation when the other captain runs into difficulties. Annie is, of course, a survivor.

Warners gave *Tugboat Annie Sails Again* a fairly

good production backing, but a better script would have improved its chances. For their fourth screen appearance together, Jane Wyman played a wealthy young socialite who falls in love with Reagan as a poor sailor. Reagan enjoyed himself as Annie's protégé, but mostly because of the time it allowed him to loll around the port of Los Angeles on location shooting. It seemed that his days of toiling in B pictures were ending.

With Alan Hale, Marjorie Rambeau and Hedda Hopper at the premiere in Tacoma, Washington.

During a break in the filming, with Jane Wyman on location in San Pedro Harbor.

SANTA FE TRAIL

A Warner Bros. First National Picture,
Directed by Michael Curtiz,
Produced by Hal B. Wallis; Associate Producer:
  Robert Fellows,
Written by Robert Buckner,
Photographed by Sol Polito,
Music by Max Steiner,
Running time: 110 minutes.

CAST:

Jeb Stuart (Errol Flynn); *Kit Carson Halliday* (Olivia de Havilland); *John Brown* (Raymond Massey); *George Armstrong Custer* (Ronald Reagan); *Tex Bell* (Alan Hale); *Bob Halliday* (William Lundigan); *Rader* (Van Heflin); *Jason Brown* (Gene Reynolds); *Cyrus Halliday* (Henry O'Neill); *Windy Brody* (Guinn [Big Boy] Williams); *Oliver Brown*

With Moroni Olsen, Frank Wilcox, David Bruce, George Haywood, Errol Flynn, and William Lundigan

With William Marshall, Errol Flynn, David Bruce, William Lundigan and Van Heflin.

110

(Alan Baxter); *Martin John Litel* (John Litel); *Robert E. Lee* (Morini Olsen); *Phil Sheridan* (David Bruce); *Barber Doyle* (Hobart Cavanaugh); *Major Sumner* (Charles D. Brown); *Kitzmiller* (Joseph Sawyer); *James Longstreet* (Frank Wilcox); *Townsley* (Ward Bond); *Shoubel Morgan* (Russell Simpson); *Gentry* (Charles Middleton); *Jefferson Davis* (Erville Anderson); *Conductor* (Spencer Charters); *Charlotte* (Suzanne Carnahan, later Susan Peters); *George Pickett* (William Marshall); *John Hood* (George Haywood); *Weiner* (Wilfred Lucas); *J. Boyce Russell* (Russell Hicks).

Getting fourth billing in *Santa Fe Trail* was another step in the right career direction for Ronald Reagan. It guaranteed wide exposure in a handsomely produced Errol Flynn adventure picture, although Reagan's role as "the best friend of the hero" was certain to be overshadowed by the film's superstar. It required Reagan to lose the female romantic lead (Olivia de Havilland), but it allowed him to later find "the right girl" (Susan Peters) and share in the heroics.

With Olivia de Havilland and Errol Flynn.

With Errol Flynn and Olivia de Havilland.

With Gene Reynolds and Errol Flynn.

With Moroni Olsen and Errol Flynn.

Santa Fe Trail is one of Hollywood's curious forays into American history. It has the look of a western, and yet it has nothing to do with cowboys, Indians, wagon trains or ranching. It never goes beyond Kansas, nor does the film have much to do with the Santa Fe Trail. It is basically about the abolitionist crusade of John Brown in the years just prior to the Civil War, and the successful campaign to track him down and hang him. The film vacillates politically between being conservative in its support of government and army policies, yet liberal in viewing a man's efforts to free the slaves. Brown, as played by Raymond Massey, appears somewhat demented in his dedication. At his hanging (the finale of the film) an officer comments, "So perish all such enemies of the Union," a puzzling epitaph considering that Brown was attempting what Abraham Lincoln succeeded with in the next decade.

The oddities of *Santa Fe Trail* do not end with its historical views. Scenarist Robert Buckner took a number of the most famous names in American mil-

With Errol Flynn, Olivia de Havilland and Susan Peters.

113

With Alan Hale, Guinn Williams and Errol Flynn.

succeeds. The direction of the masterly Michael Curtiz, the fine editing and pacing, the large cast of splendid characters, and the Steiner score all contribute to two hours of good entertainment.

According to Buckner's screenplay, Stuart and Custer are assigned to the Second United States Cavalry, stationed at Fort Leavenworth, Kansas. There they both fall in love with Kit Halliday (de Havilland), the daughter of a frontier businessman (Henry O'Neill). The job of patrolling the frontier brings them into conflict with John Brown, his family and his followers. In his attempts to free the slaves, Brown causes bloodshed and bitterness. To make his campaigns more tactical Brown hires a cashiered West Point cadet (Van Heflin), which causes the army increasing concern. But it is this same ex-cadet who, presumably in the name of patriotism, but perhaps to save his own skin, informs on Brown and reports his final movements to the army. When Brown takes over the town of Harpers Ferry, Virginia, a military force under the command of Colonel Robert E. Lee (Morini Olsen) (historically correct) is sent to defeat him. Stuart, under white flag, is ordered to confer with Brown, but when the fanatical abolitionist, calling for help from God, refuses to surrender, he is attacked and his forces beaten. He is then tried for treason and hanged. When last seen, Stuart and Custer are on a train, with Stuart being wed to Kit, as the sound track closes with Steiner's dramatic variations on "John Brown's Body."

Ronald Reagan acquitted himself well in *Santa Fe Trail,* bringing his likable qualities to Custer's invented friendship with Stuart and to his unrequited love for the character played by de Havilland. His horsemanship was of considerable help in making the film. Reagan discovered the charming swashbuckler Flynn to be a problem personality when working. Strangely, for all his charisma, Flynn was insecure about being upstaged, and constantly jockeyed for the most prominent positions in camera setups, particularly with actors who were also playing heroes, as was Reagan. "Errol was a strange person, terribly unsure of himself and needlessly so. He was a beautiful piece of machinery, likable, with great charm, and yet convinced he lacked ability as an actor. As a result, he was conscious every minute of scenes favoring other actors and their position on the screen in relation to himself. He was apparently unaware of his own striking personality."

itary history and lumped them together as comrades. Errol Flynn is seen as the Virginian gentleman J. E. B. Stuart, who would become the Confederacy's most renowned cavalry commander, but there was no effort by the actor or in the screenplay to present an accurate depiction of Stuart. Regan's casting as George Armstrong Custer is also mysterious. The film opens, accurately, with Stuart's graduation from West Point in 1854, but also shows Custer receiving his commission. In actual fact, Custer was a fifteen-year-old Ohio schoolboy at that time. Stuart and he were Civil War adversaries and never met. The movie also falsely parades Philip Sheridan, James Longstreet, George Pickett, and James Hood (all Civil War generals) as 1854 graduates. As a history lesson, *Santa Fe Trail* is highly dubious stuff. It can only be looked upon as an adventure yarn, and on those terms it fully-

THE BAD MAN

An MGM Picture,
Directed by Richard Thorpe,
Produced by J. Walter Ruben,
Written by Wells Root, based on a story by Porter
    Emerson Browne,
Photographed by Clyde De Vinna,

Running time: 70 minutes.

CAST:
Lopez (Wallace Beery); *Uncle Henry Jones* (Lionel
Barrymore); *Lucia Pell* (Larraine Day); *Gil Jones*
(Ronald Reagan); *Mr. Hardy* (Henry Travers); *Mor-*

With Laraine Day.

gan Pell (Tom Conway); *Red Giddings* (Chill Wills); *Angela Hardy* (Nydia Westman); *Pedro* (Chris-Pin Martin); *Venustiano* (Charles Stevens).

In the three years or so that Ronald Reagan had worked in Hollywood he had appeared in twenty-three films, all for Warners. The studio had no cause to loan him to other companies until late 1939, when MGM asked for his services as the young lead in *The Bad Man.* Reagan's work in *Knute Rockne—All American,* and *Santa Fe Trail* had increased his marquee value to the point where he was now considered an asset in the "young leading man" category. The pity, then, is that he was not borrowed for a vehicle better than *The Bad Man.*

Holbrook Blinn, who had been the star of Porter Emerson Browne's play, appeared as the title character in the 1923 filming, but the role went to Walter Huston for the talkie version in 1930. A decade later, MGM revived the script for their principal character actor, Wallace Beery, who had gradually become his own caricature. Since *The Bad Man* is about a lovable Mexican bandit named Pancho Lopez, it is difficult not to compare the film with Beery's well liked *Viva Villa!* (1934). The latter film does not compare favorably, as Pancho Villa was a controversial but substantial man, whereas Pancho Lopez is little more than a buffoon.

Lopez is a blustering border bandit who briefly dons the Robin Hood guise in order to help a young man, Gil Jones (Reagan), who once saved his life. Jones and his wheelchair-ridden Uncle Henry (Lionel Barrymore) face the possible loss of their ranch due to failure to meet the mortgage. Gil's childhood sweetheart Lucia (Larraine Day) arrives at the ranch with her husband (Tom Conway) for a visit. They are not a happy couple, and when Lopez arrives with his band of cattle rustlers, the old bandit decides to take matters into his own hands. He raises the money for the mortgage and sends the husband packing, leaving the girl free to pick up her romance with Gil.

The Bad Man is all Beery and a yard wide. He struts around spouting his views on law and life, and badgers his captives in growling pidgin English. He is run a close second by Barrymore, who fumes and rants at the bandits when they burst into his home in a similar manner to the scene of the gangster intruders of *Key Largo* (1948).

For Ronald Reagan, the pleasure of working on *The Bad Man* came from the experience of working with Beery and Barrymore, although both were

With Lionel Barrymore.

With Lionel Barrymore, Laraine Day, Tom Conway, Wallace Beery and Chris-Pin Martin.

With Wallace Beery, Lionel Barrymore and Laraine Day.

With Lionel Barrymore and Wallace Beery.

scene stealers. Beery was invariably the genial cur- mudgeon on the screen, but in person, he was sim- ply a curmudgeon. Director Richard Thorpe ad- vised Reagan on how to conduct himself with the vets, and warned him not to be dismayed if Beery stormed off the set in anger when things didn't go his way. On the other hand, Barrymore, who was frequently the personification of crotchetiness on film, was far more agreable in person, although still dangerous.

Says Reagan, "I had been warned about Beery, but no one had said anything about Barrymore. Let me make one thing plain—it was a great honor to work with him, and I'm glad I had the opportunity. Wally never rehearsed a line the way he would say it in the scene, so you were always on edge trying to anticipate a cue for your own line. Lionel was, of course, theatre through and through, and you were made better by his great ability—provided you kept from being run over. He was confined to his wheel- chair at the time and he could whip that contrivance around on a dime. It's hard to smile in a scene when your foot has been run over and your shin is bleed- ing from a hubcap blow."

With Tom Conway, Lionel Barrymore and Laraine Day.

MILLION DOLLAR BABY

A Warner Bros. Picture,
Directed by Curtis Bernhardt,
Produced by Hal B. Wallis,
Associate Producer: Davis Lewis,
Written by Casey Robinson, Richard Macaulay and
 Jerry Wald, based on a story by Leonard
 Spigelgass,
Photographed by Charles Rosher,
Music by Frederick Hollander,
Running time: 102 minutes.

CAST:

Pamela McAllister (Priscilla Lane); *James Amory* (Jeffrey Lynn); *Peter Rowan* (Ronald Reagan); *Cornelia Wheelwright* (May Robson); *Josie LaRue* (Lee Patrick); *Mrs. Galloway* (Helen Westley); *Simpson* (Walter Catlett); *George* (Richard Carle); *Marlin* (George Barbier); *Dr. Patterson* (John Qualen); *Mrs. Grayson* (Fay Helm); *Flo* (Nan Wynn); *Ollie Ward* (John Ridgely); *Diana Bennett* (Maris Wrixon); *Alvie Grayson* (Johnny Sheffield); *Tony*

With Priscilla Lane.

With Helen Westley and May Robson.

The film gets most of its value from the performance of May Robson, who died the following year at the age of seventy-seven. Her forte was the domineering, but essentially kindly, old lady, and in *Million Dollar Baby* she fully exercised her talent. Reagan and the other members of the cast appreciated working with her, although his chief recollection of the film was the time spent in trying to master keyboard technique. As a man with no musical experience, Reagan went to the Warner music department for two weeks and worked with a dummy keyboard and a real pianist. "A lot of acting is imitation anyway, and I became pretty good, as long as the piano remained silent. For a while there I almost convinced myself I could play."

(George Humbert); *Callahan* (James Burke); *Anna* (Greta Meyer); *Phyllis* (Jean Ames).

Perhaps the time spent working at MGM, which Ronald Reagan describes as the Tiffany of Hollywood (in contrast to the "meat and potatoes" atmosphere of Warners), lifted his confidence. His performance in *Million Dollar Baby,* on his return to home base, was spirited and pleasing. The script, with the esteemed Casey Robinson heading the writing team, allowed Reagan several deft and witty lines as a struggling concert pianist. It was based on a story by Leonard Spigelgass called "Miss Wheelwright Discovers America," and with the redoubtable May Robson as Miss Wheelwright, moviegoers of 1941 received an amusing picture.

The plot: a young attorney (Jeffrey Lynn) visits millionairess Cornelia Wheelwright, who has been living abroad for the past thirty years, and reveals to her that her late father obtained his vast fortune by defrauding his partner. Faced with the unpleasant truth, she decides to visit America and make restitution. She meets the granddaughter (Priscilla Lane) of the partner and, in order to get to know the girl, moves into the same modest rooming house. Miss Wheelwright makes a gift of a million dollars to the girl, who becomes confused and delighted. What disturbs her happiness, though, is rejection by her pianist boyfriend (Reagan), who does not want to benefit through money-by-marriage. Somewhat improbably, the love of the scrupulous musician is won back when the girl donates all her money to charity. In the meantime, the decent old woman meets a wide range of average Americans and broadens her own life.

With Priscilla Lane and Jeffrey Lynn.

119

With Priscilla Lane.

With Priscilla Lane and May Robson.

With May Robson and Priscilla Lane.

NINE LIVES ARE NOT ENOUGH

A Warner Bros. Picture,
Directed by A. Edward Sutherland,
Produced by William Jacobs,
Screenplay by Fred Niblo, Jr., based on the novel by
  Jerome Odlum,

Photographed by Ted McCord,
 Running time: 63 minutes.

CAST:
Matt Sawyer (Ronald Reagan); *Jane Abbott* (Joan

With James Gleason.

With Mary Brodel.

Perry); *Sergeant Daniels* (James Gleason); *Roy Slocum* (Peter Whitney); *Rose Chadwick* (Faye Emerson); *Murray* (Howard da Silva); *Slattery* (Edward Brophy); *Snapper Lucas* (Charles Drake); *Mrs. Slocum* (Vera Lewis); *Moxie Karper* (Ben Welden); *Colonel Andrews* (Howard Hickman); *Charles* (Tom Stevenson); *Mechanic* (John Ridgely); *Hot-Foot* (Paul Phillips); *Buckley* (Cliff Clark); *Doctor Lynen* (Walter Soderling); *Yates* (Joseph Crehan).

The role of a brash young newspaperman was one that seemed to fit Ronald Reagan like a glove—or rather, like the hat-on-the-back-of-the-head that was Hollywood's picture of a reporter in the thirties and forties. Reagan laughs, "You could always count on me to rush into a room, grab a phone and yell, 'Give me the city desk—I've got a story that will crack this town wide open.'" This was the Regan persona in *Nine Lives Are Not Enough,* in which he plays a reporter with boundless energy and dauntless curiosity.

Matt Sawyer (Reagan) writes an expose of a gangster (Ben Welden), who manages to clear himself and slap the newspaper with a libel suit. Sawyer is demoted to the police beat by his tough boss (Howard da Silva). The two policemen to whom he is assigned (James Gleason and Edward Brophy) trust him, and help him prove the gangster's guilt. They find the body of a missing millionaire, who everyone believes has committed suicide. Sawyer reports it to his paper as a murder and they print it, but the coroner insists it is a case of suicide and the reporter is fired. This only serves to make Sawyer more determined to solve the case. With the aid of his police chums and the daughter (Joan Perry) of the late millionaire, he survives attempts on his life and finally proves that the millionaire was murdered by his partner (Howard Hickman), in league with the very racketeer whom Sawyer had exposed.

The frantically paced *Nine Lives Are Not Enough* ends with the millionaire's daughter buying the newspaper, giving Sawyer (with whom she is now in love) the job as editor, and assigning the former editor to the lonely-hearts column. The film is an excellent B product, with a brisk script by Fred Niblo, Jr., and adept direction from the veteran Eddie Sutherland, who began his Hollywood career in 1914 and kept it going for fifty years. He always believed that a movie should move, which may account for Reagan being complimented by the *Variety* reviewer for giving a "superbly helter-skelter performance."

With Cliff Clark, Howard Hickman and Joan Perry.

With Edward Brophy, James Gleason and Vera Lewis.

With Peter Whitney, Vera Lewis, Edward Brophy and James Gleason.

With Joan Perry, James Gleason and Charles Drake.

With Edward Brophy, James Gleason, Joseph Crehan, Howard da Silva and Joan Perry.

INTERNATIONAL SQUADRON

A Warner Bros. Picture,
Directed by Lothar Mendes,
Produced by Edmund Grainger,
Written by Barry Trivers and Kenneth Gamet, based
  upon a play by Frank Wead,
Photographed by James Van Trees and Ted McCord,
Running time: 87 minutes.

CAST:
Jimmy Grant (Ronald Reagan); *Charles Wyatt* (James Stephenson); *Jeanette* (Olympe Bradna); *Reg Wilkins* (William Lundigan); *Connie* (Joan Perry); *Mary* (Julie Bishop); *Michele Edme* (Tod Andrews); *Omaha McGrath* (Cliff Edwards); *Bill Torrence* (John Ridgely); *Saunders* (Selmer Jackson); *Chief* (Addison Richards); *Sir Basil Wryxton*

With Olympe Bradna.

(Holmes Herbert); *Greek Waiter* (Eddy Conrad); *Major Fresney* (Crauford Kent).

It is impossible not to compare *International Squadron* with *A Yank in the R.A.F.*, released only two months prior, because it is largely the same yarn—that of a daring, capable, cocky and wise-cracking American who joins the Royal Air Force and learns respect for the British. The difference is mostly one of budget, with the frugal Warner Bros. scrimping on production costs, even to the extent of raiding their own script files. The basis of *International Squadron* is the 1935 James Cagney film *Ceiling Zero*, which was based on a play by aviator-turned-writer Frank Wead. In the Cagney version, he was a daredevil pilot whose irresponsible antics caused the death of a fellow pilot, for which he atoned by sacrificing his own life in testing new flight equipment.

In the Reagan version, he is a crack stunt pilot who accepts the job of flying a bomber to England, to deliver it to the RAF. Once there, he finds two old friends in British uniform, one a squadron commander (James Stephenson) and the other a fighter pilot (William Lundigan). They try to persuade him to join the service but the fun-loving Yank shows no interest. However, that night he undergoes an air raid in London, during which he sees a child killed which causes a change of heart and he resolves to help defeat the Nazis.

The Yank takes a liking to the sweetheart (Olympe Bradna) of a French pilot (Tod Andrews). He becomes so smitten with the girl that he fails to report for a patrol mission and his American friend substitutes for him and is killed in action. This brings the Yank, who has already alienated many of the other pilots with his cavalier manners, to his senses and he decides to atone. When the French pilot is assigned to a dangerous bombing mission, the Yank knocks him out and takes his place. He carries out the job and takes on several German fighter planes, ending in a fiery but heroic death.

International Squadron is typical wartime entertainment, with fairly good action sequences and an appropriately breezy performance by Reagan as the cocksure American. A few reviewers commented that it was his best role. The film is a reminder that the RAF did indeed have several squadrons of men from various European countries and the United States, many of whom helped to increase the romantic wartime mystique of the Royal Air Force's Fighter Command. The picture was the last for the

With Cliff Edwards.

With Reginald Denny.

With Olympe Bradna.

With James Stephenson (addressing the pilots).

agreeable British actor James Stephenson, who died at the age of fifty-three after completing this film. Stephenson had made a fine impression with his role opposite Bette Davis in *The Letter,* and he was next slated to appear with Reagan in *Kings Row* as Dr. Tower, a part which Claude Rains was later called upon to take.

The studios usually had the cooperation of the airplane manufacturers for the use of craft in making most wartime pictures. With the Lockheed plant only two miles up the street from Warners, the studio could use Hudson bombers, which is why that particular airplane appeared in so many Warner pictures. But in the case of securing British and German aircraft, the producers had access to stock footage and for close-ups, they invented some odd aircraft. *International Squadron* drew laughs when shown in England, because of the fighter plane flown by Reagan. "Our 'Spitfire' was a doctored-up Ryan monoplane that didn't even have retractable gear."

With Helmut Dantine (behind Reagan) and James Stephenson.

James Stephenson, left of Reagan, and William Lundigan to the right.

KINGS ROW

A Warner Bros. Picture,
Directed by Sam Wood,
Produced by Hal B. Wallis,
Written by Casey Robinson, based on the novel by
  Henry Bellamann,
Photographed by James Wong Howe,
Music by Erich Wolfgang Korngold,
Running time: 127 minutes.

CAST:
Randy Monoghan (Ann Sheridan); *Parris Mitchell* (Robert Cummings); *Drake McHugh* (Ronald Reagan); *Dr. Henry Gordon* (Charles Coburn); *Cassandra Tower* (Betty Field); *Dr. Alexander Tower* (Claude Rains); *Mrs. Gordon* (Judith Anderson); *Louise Gordon* (Nancy Coleman); *Elise Sandor* (Karen Verne); *Madame Von Eln* (Maria Ouspenskaya); *Colonel Skeffington* (Harry Davenport); *Pa Monoghan* (Ernest Cossart); *Tom Monoghan* (Pat Moriarty); *Ann* (Ilka Grunning); *Sam Winters* (Minor Watson); *Doctor Berdoff* (Ludwig Stossel); *Mr. Sandor* (Erwin Kalser); *Doctor Candell* (Egon

With Robert Cummings.

With Robert Cummings.

With Julie Warren, Mary Scott and Robert Cummings.

Brecher); *Randy as a child* (Ann Todd); *Parris as a child* (Scotty Beckett); *Drake as a child* (Douglas Croft); *Cassandra as a child* (Mary Thomas); *Louise as a child* (Joan Duval).

Kings Row is the most distinguished film of Ronald Reagan's career and the one which drew him the most favorable response. It is not at all typical of the Hollywood product of its time, dealing as it does with the darker side of human behavior. The casting of Reagan, Ann Sheridan and Robert Cummings in the leads raised eyebrows within the industry. They were all amiable players of light material but were not the obvious choices to play the characters in Henry Bellamann's massive story of sadism, suicide and thwarted love in a small, turn-of-the-century American town. And yet, what emerged on the screen was, and is, a film masterpiece. It was the turning point for Ronald Reagan that every actor awaits—one that elevates him to respect and serious consideration. Unfortunately for Reagan, by the time the film was released, he was in the Army and hardly in a position to take advantage of his new position. More than four years would go by before he was able to resume his screen career. Because of *Kings Row* he would be welcomed back by his employers and the public but it is unhappy that so much career momemtum was lost due to his absence.

The actual Bellamann novel barely made it to the screen. A great deal of its thematic substance dealt with matters rated as unacceptable to the Motion Picture Production Code, matters such as incest, homosexuality and euthanasia. Warners bought the rights to the story in 1940 for $35,000 and assigned ace screen writer Casey Robinson to attempt an adaptation. Robinson was appalled and finally threw the book aside. It then occurred to him how to solve the novel's primary censorship hurdle, which was its theme of incest in relationship between Doctor Tower and his daughter Cassandra. Robinson decided to make it a matter of insanity, with the doctor unable to cure the girl. Robinson conferred with producer Hal B. Wallis, who agreed and told him to proceed with his version of the story. Robinson toned down some of the more macabre aspects of the novel, such as Parris Mitchell, the principle character, affecting a mercy killing of his grandmother; and in the case of Drake McHugh (the role played by Reagan) Robinson invented a new ending. In the novel Drake dies of cancer as the result of losing both legs in an unnecessary am-

129

With Nancy Coleman and Robert Cummings.

With Ann Sheridan, Pat Moriarty and Ernest Cossart.

putation. Robinson decided on a more optimistic course, with Drake emerging from his mental depression and resolving to pick up his life.

The film begins with a group of children making their way home from school. Parris takes his sweetheart Cassandra swimming and then goes home to his elegant grandmother (Maria Ouspenskaya), who reminds him that he has invitations to two parties—Cassandra's and the one being given by Doctor and Mrs. Henry Gordon (Charles Coburn and Judith Anderson) for their daughter, Louise. Parris decides to go to Cassandra's party, knowing that she

is considered strange by the other children and that her affair will be poorly attended. Later Parris and Drake go to the railroad yards and swing on the rings in the icehouse. They are joined by the tomboyish Randy Monoghan. On his way home Parris is approached by Cassandra, who tells him that her father, Doctor Tower (Claude Rains), has taken her out of school and that she will no longer be able to see him.

A dozen years pass and the five children grow up. Parris (Robert Cummings) has become a fine young gentleman and a medical student, who takes private instruction from Doctor Tower. Cassandra (Betty Field) is now a pretty but sheltered neurotic. Louise (Nancy Coleman) is repressed by her harsh parents, and severely warned against seeing the playboy Drake (Reagan), who exists handsomely on an inherited allowance. One day he encounters Randy (Ann Sheridan), who, having grown into a lovely but practical working class girl, chides him about his roguish ways and gradually falls in love with him, to the consternation of Louise.

On one of his visits to the Tower home, Parris sees Cassandra, and their love for each other renews itself. But great sorrow is about to enter Parris' life—his grandmother dies of cancer. He is about to leave town in order to study medicine in

With Ann Sheridan and Ernest Cossart.

Vienna, but he is loath to leave Cassandra. She begs to go with him, but he delays in answering her. The next day, he learns that she has been killed by her father and that he has thereafter taken his own life. An investigation shows that Doctor Tower had considered his daughter incurably insane, like her mother, but an autopsy reveals that Cassandra had been pregnant.

Parris is seen off to Vienna by Drake and Randy, who are by this time very pleased with each other's company. But trouble is now about to strike Drake. He finds that a bank embezzlement has robbed him of his funds. He swallows his pride and asks Randy's father, a railroad yard foreman (Ernest Cossart), for a job. Louise becomes bitter toward her parents for keeping her from the man she loves. One night while working in the rail yards, Drake is hit by a falling pile of boxes and is thrown in the path of a train. Doctor Gordon is called in and makes the decision that both legs must be amputated.

Parris returns to Kings Row after completing his studies. He finds a despondent Drake being treated with great love and devotion by Randy, and an almost demented Louise, cursing the name of her recently deceased father. It becomes apparent that Doctor Gordon had amputated Drake's legs unnecessarily as a form of punishment for the young man's formerly hedonistic ways. Parris visits his former home and finds it occupied by a Viennese doctor (Erwin Kalser) and his lovely daughter (Karen Verne). She and Parris soon fall in love, and, having found his own happiness, Parris decides to help Drake and Randy. He tells Drake the truth in the most direct manner. Drake vows that Doctor Gordon will not be responsible for ruining his life. He promises Randy that he'll do all the things she has planned for them.

With Ann Sheridan.

With Ann Sheridan.

Kings Row remains a classic, and one which does not lose its impact with time. The direction of film veteran Sam Wood is firm and unwavering. The cast is, for the most part, superb. Actors such as Rains, Coburn, Anderson and Ouspenskaya give performances that are reminders of Hollywood at its cogent best. The younger actors, particularly Reagan, Betty Fields and Ann Sheridan, made a fine impression on both the critics and the public, although there were those who felt Robert Cummings should have been more forceful. Warner Bros. had wanted Tyrone Power for the part, but 20th Century-Fox refused to loan him to the studio.

Kings Row benefited from the contributions of three legendary film artists: cinemaphotographer James Wong Howe, whose black-and-white images are finely contrasted; production designer William Cameron Menzies, whose every set is a vivid part of the technique of telling a story on film; and Erich

131

Wolfgang Korngold, whose full-bodied score is an example of quality dramatic composition. Because of the work of these three men, *Kings Row* is an essential item in film study.

Ronald Reagan was only one of the actors Warner Bros. considered for the role of Drake McHugh. Among those under contract to the studio were Dennis Morgan, Jack Carson and Jeffrey Lynn, and Eddie Albert. Robert Preston and Franchot Tone were also considered. The studio finally decided on Reagan, whom they wanted to build into a market value. He was ideal for the role of Drake, the rather cocky but charming man-around-town, and the test came when he portrayed the character as a bitter and depressed victim of misfortune. He handled the role well, and recalls, "It was a long, hard schedule and my first experience, I suppose, with an acting chore that got down inside and kind of wrung me out."

Reagan's main recollection of *Kings Row* is the gratitude he felt toward director Sam Wood, particularly in shooting the famous scene where Drake McHugh awakens after his operation and realizes he is without his legs. He yells, "Where's the rest of me?" It was the line he chose to use as a title of his autobiography, and a line that some of his political opponents have used as a snide reference to his abilities in politics.

The crucial scene was one which Reagan almost dreaded doing, since it was intensely dramatic and could slip into the ludicrous if played carelessly. He sweated about it for weeks and rehearsed in a variety of ways. He questioned doctors, psychiatrists and paraplegics. The night before the scene was scheduled to be shot, Reagan could not sleep. He

With Robert Cummings and Ann Sheridan.

came to the set the following morning looking haggard and was still unsure of how to deliver the line. He climbed into the dummy bed, with its holes in the mattress for his legs, and spent a dismal hour staring down at the smooth space where his legs should have been. In his autobiography he recalls: "Gradually the affair began to terrify me. In some weird way, I felt something horrible had happened to my body. Then gradually I became aware that the crew had quietly assembled, the camera was in position, and the set all lighted. Sam Wood, the director, stood beside me, watching me sweat.

" 'Want to shoot it?' he said in a low voice.

" 'No rehearsal?' I begged. Somehow I knew this one had to be for real.

"God rest his soul, fine director that he was, he just turned to the crew and said, 'Let's make it.'

"There were cries of 'Lights!' and 'Quiet please!' I lay back and closed my eyes, as tense as a fiddlestring. I heard Sam's low voice call, 'Action!' There was the sharp *clack* which signaled the beginning of the scene. I opened my eyes dazedly, looked around, slowly let my gaze travel downward. I can't describe even now my feelings as I tried to reach for where my legs should be. 'Randy!' I screamed. Ann Sheridan (bless her), burst through the door. She wasn't in the shot, and normally wouldn't have been on hand until we turned the camera around to get her entrance, but she knew it was one of those scenes where a fellow actor needed all the help he could get and at that moment, in my mind, she was Randy answering my call. I asked the question—the words that had been haunting me for so many weeks—'Where's the rest of me?'

"There was no retake. It was a good scene and it came out that way in the picture. Perhaps I never did quite as well again in a single shot."

With Ann Sheridan.

JUKE GIRL

A Warner Bros. Picture,
Directed by Curtis Bernhardt,
Produced by Hal B. Wallis,
Associate Producers: Jerry Wald and Jack Saper,
Written by A. I. Bezzerides, adapted by Kenneth
  Gamet from a story by Theodore Pratt,
Photographed by Bert Glennon,
Music by Adolph Deutsch,
Running time: 90 minutes.

CAST:
Lola Mears (Ann Sheridan); *Steve Talbot* (Ronald Reagan); *Danny Frazier* (Richard Whorf); *Nick Garcos* (George Tobias); *Henry Madden* (Gene Lockhart); *Yippee* (Alan Hale); *Skeeter* (Betty Brewer); *Muckeye John* (Howard da Silva); *Just* (Willard Robinson); *Violet Murphy* (Faye Emerson); *Jo-Mo* (Willie Best); *Ike Harper* (Fuzzy Knight); *Keene* (Spencer Charters); *Paley* (William Davidson); *Truck Driver* (Frank Wilcox); *Watchman* (William Haade).

Juke Girl was not much of a reward to Ronald Reagan and Ann Sheridan for their excellent work in *Kings Row*. Within a few days of finishing the romance and somber elegance of the Bellamann story, the actors were roughly transported to the world of itinerant crop pickers in Florida, and the ugly conflicts between management and labor. *Juke Girl*, the title of which barely hints at its content, may be regarded as a truck farmer's version of *The Grapes of Wrath*.

In this grimy melodrama, a pair of drifters, Steve (Reagan) and Danny (Richard Whorf) arrive in Florida and pick up work in the tomato fields. Their friendship becomes strained when a dispute erupts between the owner (Gene Lockhart) of a fruit farm and packing plant, and a farmer (George Tobias), who bitterly resents the low prices paid for his crops. Steve sides with the farmer and Danny sees his opportunities with the owner. The tense local situation comes to a head one night in a juke joint, where girls are employed to entertain the field workers. The anger over low wages and long hours

With Ann Sheridan.

With Ann Sheridan.

With Ann Sheridan and George Tobias.

**With Alan Hale, Richard Whorf, Howard da Silva,
Faye Emerson and Gene Lockhart.**

134

explodes into a vicious brawl. One of the girls (Sheridan) joins with Steve in his campaign for the farmers. Together they set out to break the monopoly of the packing house owner. They achieve their goal, but only after killings, violence, commercial intrigue and moments of mob justice and destruction.

Juke Girl is a disturbing reminder of the plight of farm workers forty years ago and presents relatively realistic views of Florida farm field operations. The film contains much brawling and roughhouse tactics, most of which involves tomatoes being used as weapons. As Reagan remembers the location shooting, it was uncomfortable and sometimes unsanitary. Much of the shooting was done during the winter of 1941-1942 in California farmlands, where the temperature frequently neared freezing, even though the story was supposed to take place in the sticky humidity of Florida. The script called for night exterior shots, forcing the

Gene Lockhart receiving tomato.

With George Tobias and Richard Whorf.

With Howard da Silva and Ann Sheridan.

With Faye Emerson, Ann Sheridan and Richard Whorf.

actors to smoke to disguise their vaporized breath in the cold night air. Glycerin was sprayed on their faces to simulate sweat.

The biggest fight scene in *Juke Girl* involves a horde of management-hired thugs smashing up truck loads of crated tomatoes waiting to be shipped to market by the independent farmers. For three nights Reagan and his fellow sufferers wallowed in squashed tomatoes, which were shovelled back into their crates at the end of the shots and reused in the next scenes. The smell and dampness combined to make this filming a low point of Reagan's years as an actor, but his biggest problem in *Juke Girl* was one of simple exhaustion. The picture would have been a back-breaker, even if Reagan and Sheridan had had plenty of rest and a fresh start, but coming directly after the long months of hard work on *Kings Row*, it proved to be a great strain. "I discovered how nervous fatigue can creep up on you. On the night shift, going to work at 6:00 P.M., we shot night exteriors until sunup for thirty-eight nights. With all the misconceptions about pampered stars, none is so far afield as the belief that physical discomfort isn't tolerated."

136

DESPERATE JOURNEY

A Warner Bros. First National Picture,
Directed by Raoul Walsh,
Produced by Hal B. Wallis,
Associate Producer: Jack Saper,
Written by Arthur T. Horman,
Photographed by Bert Glennon,
Music by Max Steiner,
Running time: 107 minutes.

CAST:
Flight Lieutenant Terrence Forbes (Errol Flynn);
Flying Officer Johnny Hammond (Ronald Reagan);
Kaethe Brahms (Nancy Coleman); *Major Otto Bau-meister* (Raymond Massey); *Flight Sergeant Kirk Edwards* (Alan Hale); *Flying Officer Jed Forrest* (Arthur Kennedy); *Flight Sergeant Lloyd Hollis* (Ronald Sinclair); *Doctor Mather* (Albert Basser-

With Alan Hale.

With Douglas Walton (standing).

man); *Preuss* (Sig Rumann); *Squadron Leader Lane Ferris* (Patrick O'Moore); *Dr. Herman Brahms* (Felix Basch); *Frau Brahms* (Ilka Gruning); *Frau Raeder* (Elsa Basserman); *Captain Coswick* (Charles Irwin); *Squadron Leader Clark* (Richard Fraser); *Kruse* (Robert O. Davis); *Heinrich Schwartzmuller* (Henry Victor); *Assistant Plotting Officer* (Bruce Lester); *Wing Commander* (Lester Matthews); *Hesse* (Kurt Katch); *Gestapo Man* (Hans Schumm); *German Copilot* (Helmut Dantine); *Squadron Commander* (Barry Bernard).

Even at the time of its release, *Desperate Journey* was a preposterous war movie. It is the kind of film which presents the German military of the Second World War as such nincompoops that the viewer is left wondering why it took the Allies so long to bring the war to an end. Of the five films Errol Flynn made about that war, this is by far the most implausible. It can only be viewed as a Rover Boys yarn, and as such it is, thanks largely to the brisk direction of Raoul Walsh, fairly good entertainment. By this time in his career, Ronald Reagan was enough of a star to receive cobilling with Flynn, although still having to fight for a proper balance in the script. Flynn didn't mind having a heroine as a costar, but another *hero* was a different story.

Desperate Journey is the tale of the adventures of an RAF bomber on a mission to Germany, and the producers overdid their attempts to please as many nationalities as possible. Here Flynn is an Australian pilot, Arthur Kennedy is a Canadian navigator, Alan Hale is a Scottish veteran of the first World War (who would in fact have been too old for combat flying), Ronald Sinclair is an Englishman, and Ronald Reagan is that most popular of war movie characters—a Yank in the RAF—brash, amusing, irreverent, pragmatic and brave. It was as if the Secret Service's Brass Bancroft had joined in the fight against the Nazis, and found it a pushover.

The crew of the RAF Flying Fortress D-for-Danny take flight, after much good-natured bantering at the briefing, for a bombing run over Germany. Upon dropping their bombs, they are shot down and tracked by a German army unit under Major Otto Baumeister (Raymond Massey). The major is in charge of a secret Messerschmidt plant. The lads easily outwit the major and escape, making their way across wartime Germany as they head for the north coast. They engage in sabotage and various acts of violent conflict, which diminishes their number to a band of three survivors—the Aus-

With Alan Hale, Arthur Kennedy, Ronald Sinclair and Errol Flynn.

With Errol Flynn, Alan Hale, Arthur Kennedy, Ronald Sinclair and Raymond Massey.

tralian, the Canadian and the American. They are aided by an anti-Nazi German family headed by a genial doctor (Albert Basserman), who has a sweet daughter (Nancy Coleman). They inspire the allied lads to bring about the downfall of the Nazis. The boys finally reach the coast, steal a German bomber (which is, incidentally, a captured RAF Hudson), machine gun the major and his team, and take off. As they fly across the English Channel, the Australian pilot, having so easily vanquished Hitler's warriors, says, "Now for Australia and a crack at the Japs!"—a line which was to haunt Flynn the remainder of his days.

Desperate Journey is a yarn impossible to take seriously. It's comic strip stuff, but made enjoyable by good production values, not the least of which is Raymond Massey indulging himself in Germanic villainy. The best scene comes early in the picture, when Massey, after having questioned the captured RAF crew, calls for a private interview with the

American Reagan, thinking the Yank more likely to respond to a gentlemanly chat. The Yank does indeed agree to reveal what he knows about the new RAF bomber engines, and reels off an impressive string of facts about the component parts—all nonsense. Once he has the major's rapt attention, he punches him on the jaw, knocking him out, and then helps himself to the major's breakfast.

Reagan was eager to do *Desperate Journey*, but having worked with Flynn before, he was hesitant about the scene with Massey. It was the kind of cheeky scene in which Flynn specialized, and Reagan assumed he might well lose it. Had it not been for producer Hal B. Wallis, Flynn would surely have ended up doing the scene, but Wallis had promised Reagan the picture would be shot as scripted. Despite Flynn's maneuvering to the contrary, Wallis stuck to his word. After each conference Wallis would say, "Shoot it as it's written." Says Reagan, "We did just that and I'm grateful to

With Arthur Kennedy, Alan Hale, Errol Flynn and Raymond Massey.

With Ronald Sinclair, Alan Hale and Errol Flynn.

him: the scene got big laughs in the theater.''

By the time *Desperate Journey* was released in September of 1942, Reagan was in another uniform —a real one—and he would be in it for more than three years. Due to his commission in the Army reserve he was made a second lieutenant, then a first, and finally a captain. For a few weeks in 1943, Reagan was demoted to the ranks when he was ordered to appear in a wartime film called *This Is the Army.*

During a break in the filming, with Errol Flynn, stuntman Buster Wiles and Ronald Sinclair.

THIS IS THE ARMY

A Warner Bros. Picture,
Directed by Michael Curtiz,
Produced by Jack L. Warner and Hal B. Wallis,
Written by Casey Robinson and Claude Binyon,
    based on the play by Irving Berlin,
Photographed in Technicolor by Bert Glennon and
    Sol Polito,
Songs by Irving Berlin,
Musical direction by Ray Heindorf,
Running time: 121 minutes.

CAST:

Jerry Jones (George Murphy); *Eileen Dibble* (Joan Leslie); *Maxie Stoloff* (George Tobias); *Sergeant McGee* (Alan Hale); *Eddie Dibble* (Charles Butterworth); *Ethel* (Rosemary DeCamp); *Mrs. Davidson* (Dolores Costello); *Rose Dibble* (Una Merkel); *Major Davidson* (Stanley Ridges); *Mrs. O'Brien* (Ruth Donnelly); *Mrs. Nelson* (Dorothy Peterson); *Johnny Jones* (Ronald Reagan). With Kate Smith,

Joe Louis, Frances Langford, Gertrude Niesen and members of the stage production.

Musical program:
1. Overture.
2. "Your Country and My Country." Gertrude Niesen.
3. "My Sweetie." George Murphy.
4. "Poor Little Me, I'm on K. P." George Tobias and Company.
5. "We're on Our Way to France." George Murphy and Company.
6. "God Bless America." Kate Smith.
7. "What Does He Look Like?" Frances Langford.
8. "This is the Army, Mr. Jones." Company.
9. "I'm Getting Tired So I Can Sleep." James Burell.
10. "Mandy." Ralph Magelssen and Company.
11. "The Army's Made a Man Out of Me." Company.
12. "Ladies of the Chorus." Alan Hale and Company.
13. "That's What the Well-dressed Man in Harlem Will Wear." James Cross and Company.
14. "How About a Cheer for the Navy?" Company.
15. "I Left My Heart at the Stage Door Canteen." Earl Oxford.
16. "With My Head in the Clouds." Robert Shanley.
17. "American Eagles." Robert Shanley and Company.
18. "Oh, How I Hate to Get Up in the Morning." Irving Berlin.
19. "This Time is the Last Time." Robert Shanley and Company.

The original New York stage production of *This Is the Army* opened at the Broadway Theatre on July 4, 1942, and the producer was listed as one Uncle Sam. It should have read, of course, Irving Berlin, since he wrote the book, the lyrics, the music, and put the show together. Berlin persuaded the War Department to let him have three hundred men from the services to do a musical that would raise a projected one million dollars for Army Relief, a fund designed to help needy soldiers and their families. By the time the show finished touring, it had raised ten million dollars. The movie version brought in two million after Warner Bros. sub-

tracted their minimum production costs.

The uniformed talent in both the stage and screen versions of *This Is the Army* performed for service pay. Ronald Reagan received his first lieutenant's wages of about $250 a month during the time he was involved in the filming. Reagan had been in the army for a year when he was seconded to appear in the film, a pleasant duty for him, and one which took him back to his own studio. It was a relatively easy assignment, and a relief from his chores as a maker of service training films, calling for him to be the author of the show the soldiers perform in the film. As such he is the son of a show producer (George Murphy), a man who had served in the First World War. When the son completes the show, he, too, is called to the colors.

The film is an expansion of the stage production. Scenarists Casey Robinson and Claude Binyon devised a story which combined material from Irving Berlin's 1917 soldier show *Yip, Yip, Yaphank* with the new songs of Berlin's 1942 production. The story starts with a favorite star of Broadway musicals, Jerry Jones (Murphy), being drafted and put in charge of an army show. The show is a success, and at the final performance, the cast marches out of the theatre and off to actual war. At the outbreak of the second World War, Jerry is a producer on Broadway and his son Johnny (Reagan) is his assistant. History repeats itself when Johnny goes into the army. He becomes the author of *This Is the Army*. At the final performance in Washington before the President, he takes time out to marry his sweetheart (Joan Leslie). Also at that final performance, Jerry Jones and some of his chums from *Yip, Yip, Yaphank* appear to do a nostalgic number about their days in the army—together with Irving Berlin —"Oh, How I Hate to Get Up in the Morning." There is no mention of Berlin being the author of all the material in both shows, but it is hardly a point to debate. Everyone knows who wrote it. *This Is the Army* is a magnificent movie musical and one which made a unique contribution to the war effort.

Ronald Reagan was introduced to Irving Berlin a number of times during the making of the film. At one point, Berlin sought Reagan out to compliment him on a sequence he had just watched, and to give some critical advice. Berlin ended by saying, "You really should give this business some consideration when the war is over. It's very possible you could have a career in show business." Reagan thanked him but started to wonder. Was it that Berlin had

not seen any of his movies, or had the war been going on for so long that Ronald Reagan the actor was forgotten? Reagan had little time to ponder the point. As soon as his shots were finished, he was back in his lieutenant's uniform and making movies for military training.

With George Murphy, Joan Leslie and Charles Butterworth.

With Joan Leslie.

STALLION ROAD

A Warner Bros. Picture,
Directed by James V. Kern,
Produced by Alex Gottlieb,
Written by Stephen Longstreet, based on his novel,
Photographed by Arthur Edeson,
Music by Frederick Hollander,
Running time: 97 minutes.

CAST:
Larry Hanrahan (Ronald Reagan); *Rory Teller* (Alexis Smith); *Stephen Purcell* (Zachary Scott); *Daisy Otis* (Peggy Knudsen); *Chris Teller* (Patti Brady); *Doctor Stevens* (Harry Davenport); *Lana Rock* (Angela Greene); *Pelon* (Frank Puglia); *Richmond Mallard* (Ralph Byrd); *Ben Otis* (Lloyd Corrigan); *Chico* (Fernando Alvarado); *Joe Beasley* (Matthew Boulton); *Mrs. Ford* (Mary Gordon); *Maria* (Nina Campana); *Moxie* (Dewey Robinson); *Tommy* (Paul Panzer); *Beasley, Jr.* (Bobby Valentine).

With Alexis Smith.

With Zachary Scott and Frank Puglia.

With Zachary Scott and Alexis Smith.

Like so many actors returning to Hollywood after being in the services, Ronald Reagan had the problem of reminding the public that he had been a star. It was not a case of merely being employed; Warners welcomed him back and restored him to star rank. The problem was one of finding the right films for a public that had changed during the war years. Reagan found that movies were no longer ground out like sausages, and that he was required to appear in only two or three vehicles a year. It therefore became even more important to find good material.

After waiting a considerable time, Warners assigned Reagan to *Stallion Road,* which pleased him because it concerned horse ranching and would be made largely on location. Even more agreeable was the fact that it was designed for Humphrey Bogart and Lauren Bacall, and would be shot in Technicolor. But the Bogarts decided that it was not the kind of film they wanted to do, and Alexis Smith and Zachary Scott were brought in. The budget was then cut and the film was shot in black-and-white, a regrettable decision in view of the locations in the picturesque Sierra Madre Range, north of Los Angeles, with lush mountain meadows sweeping down to the coast.

Stephen Longstreet's screenplay has a novelist (Scott) examining an episode in his recent past as he contemplates writing about it. The film title refers to a horse breeding ranch of that name, owned by Larry Hanrahan (Reagan), who is also the area veterinarian. The novelist, Stephen, pays his friend Larry a visit and makes notes about his lifestyle. Larry is called upon to care for the ailing prize mare of a local rancher, Rory Teller (Smith). The horse does not appear to be very sick and a cure is immediately effected. The horse then appears at a state fair jumping contest and beats the vet's own entry, but soon after it lapses into illness and dies. Rory blames Larry for being negligent and curbs her growing love for him because he didn't answer her call for help. However, Larry is at this time engaged in trying to fight an outbreak of anthrax that has stricken a herd of cattle.

With the veterinarian busy with his problems, romance flairs up between Rory and the novelist. He takes advantage of the rift between Rory and Larry, and asks her to marry him. The anthrax plague reaches greater proportions and it becomes apparent to Rory that she was wrong in spurning Larry for not coming when she needed him. Larry perfects a serum but becomes infected with anthrax himself. His doctor (Harry Davenport) gives him up for lost, but Rory injects an unproven serum into Larry and the gamble pays off. He recovers, and their romance gains new momentum. The novelist wisely accepts the outcome.

Stallion Road is pleasant and interesting, especially the shots of horses gamboling over lush hillsides and along the spectacular California seashore. The film worked well for Reagan in terms of being a re-introduction to the public. It was not a difficult part for him, and the critics said, as they had through most of his career, that he was likable and believable. His performance allowed Warner Bros. to continue with their plans to maintain his star

With Alexis Smith.

With Zachary Scott, Patti Brady and Alexis Smith.

With Alexis Smith, Zachary Scott and Peggy Knudsen.

With Zachary Scott and Alexis Smith.

standing. *Stallion Road* did not go into production until the latter part of 1946 and involved 109 days of shooting, an unusually long period for a film of that day. After editing and the addition of Frederick Hollander's pleasant score, the film was not ready until March of 1947, almost four years after Reagan's appearance in *This Is the Army*.

The film is a favorite of Reagan's because of the involvement of horses. He was anxious to get back into the horsey life and to do his own riding and jumping in the picture. He hired a former Italian cavalry officer, Nino Pepitone, as his coach, which proved to be the start of a long friendship and partnership. Pepitone would help Reagan set up his own horse ranch, first in the San Fernando Valley, and later in the more distant Malibu Hills.

THAT HAGEN GIRL

A Warner Bros. Picture,
Directed by Peter Godfrey,
Produced by Alex Gottlieb,
Written by Charles Hoffman, based on the novel by
  Edith Roberts,
Photographed by Karl Freund,

Music by Franz Waxman,
Running time: 83 minutes.

CAST:
Tom Bates (Ronald Reagan); *Mary Hagen* (Shirley
Temple); *Ken Freneau* (Rory Calhoun); *Julia Kane*

With Douglas Kennedy.

With Lois Maxwell.

With Frank Conroy and William Edmunds.

(Lois Maxwell); *Minta Hagen* (Dorothy Peterson); *Joe Hagen* (Charles Kemper); *Dewey Coons* (Conrad Janis); *Christine Delaney* (Penny Edwards); *Sharon Bailey* (Jean Porter); *Molly Freneau* (Nella Walker); *Judge Merrivale* (Harry Davenport); *Selma Delaney* (Winnifred Harris); *Trenton Gately* (Moroni Olsen); *Doctor Stone* (Frank Conroy); *Miss Grover* (Kathryn Card); *Herb* (Douglas Kennedy); *Lorna Gately* (Barbara Brown).

That Hagen Girl is among the films of which Ronald Reagan is least proud, mostly because it put him in a role he did not like, that of a man in love with a girl half his age, but also because it did nothing to further his career at a time when it needed bolstering. The film was released one-half year after *Stallion Road*, and it did not reinforce the good impression he had made in that film. *That Hagen Girl* did even less for Shirley Temple, who had been struggling to maintain her position in Hollywood. She had gone from being an adorable child star to a rather ordinary teenage actress, and this picture did nothing to halt her decline.

The Edith Roberts novel is pure soap opera, and five scripts of it were written before it was given the go-ahead. The story revolves around old-fashioned, small town gossip. Mary Hagen (Temple) is an adoptee who hears rumors throughout her childhood and adolescence about her parentage, mostly that she is the illegitimate daughter of a demented heiress and a local war hero who has become a lawyer, Tom Bates (Reagan). Mary is befriended by a teacher (Lois Maxwell) and romanced by a young socialite, Ken (Rory Calhoun), but most of the townspeople shun her. Her foster mother (Dorothy Peterson) dies, and she is expelled from school for provoking a brawl, which was, in fact, not her fault.

Tom Bates returns to town from Washington, where he has been decorated for his war service, and he gradually falls in love with Mary, despite the rumor of him being her father. He rescues Mary from an attempt at suicide by drowning, and she accepts his proposal of marriage. To further ease her mind, Tom proves that she had actually come from an orphanage in Evanston, Illinois, and that the gossip she has heard all her life is meaningless.

The weak link in *That Hagen Girl* is the gossip, since it could presumably have been stilled at any time by the facts. Reagan tried to be released from making the picture, but having already rejected several scripts offered to him by Jack Warner, he was

With Shirley Temple.

not in a good position to bargain. Even after he had accepted the part, Reagan continued to petition the producer to have the script rewritten and let Mary end in the arms of her young boyfriend.

Reagan was at least able to have his most embarrassing line excised from the final release. He had objected to the character's declaration of love to the young girl, feeling that it was absurd. He was proven right at the sneak preview of the picture. "Came the moment on the screen when I said to Shirley, 'I love you,' and the entire audience cried, en masse, 'Oh, no!' I sat huddled in the darkness until I was sure the lobby would be empty. You couldn't have gotten me to face that audience for a million bucks. Before release the line was edited out of the picture, leaving us with a kind of oddball finish in which we climb on a train—Shirley carrying a bouquet—and leave town. You are left to guess as to whether we are married, just traveling together, or did I adopt her?''

With Harry Davenport.

151

With Shirley Temple.

THE VOICE OF THE TURTLE

A Warner Bros. Picture,
Directed by Irving Rapper,
Produced by Charles Hoffman,
Written by John Van Druten, based on his play,
Photographed by Sol Polito,
Music by Max Steiner,
Running time: 103 minutes.

CAST:
Bill Page (Ronald Reagan); *Sally Middleton* (Eleanor Parker); *Olive Lashbrook* (Eve Arden); *Ned Burling* (Wayne Morris); *Kenneth Bartlett* (Kent Smith); *George Harrington* (John Emery); *Storekeeper* (Erskine Sanford); *Henry Atherton* (John Holland); *Headwaiter* (Nino Pepitone).

With Eve Arden and Eleanor Parker.

With Wayne Morris, Eve Arden and Eleanor Parker.

When Warners bought John Van Druten's wartime play *The Voice of the Turtle*, the author was hired to write the screenplay. Since it was an intimate three-character play, it became his responsibility to broaden it for cinematic value and to add new characters. The hit play, which opened in New York in 1943, was still playing when the film opened at Christmas, 1947, and those who said the sophisticated play could not work on the screen were proved wrong.

Ronald Reagan tried to avoid doing *The Voice of the Turtle* because he felt that, although it was a pleasing comedy, it would not help his screen image. He was hoping for meatier and more dramatic material. John Huston offered him the role (which was eventually played by Bruce Bennett) in *The Treasure of the Sierra Madre*, but Jack Warner had purchased the Van Druten play with Reagan in mind, and he considered it more important than letting him play a character role in the Huston picture. Reagan had been argumentative with Warner since his return to the studio, and he sensed that refusing to do *Turtle* could cost him his contract.

Margaret Sullavan had been the star of the Broadway play but Warner Bros. used contractee Eleanor Parker, giving her a Sullavan-style haircut and encouraging a similar performance. Reagan ob-

jected at first to Parker as his costar, as she had emerged during his years away from the studio and he was not familiar with her work. He tried to persuade Warners to hire June Allyson for the part, but his persuasions, like his objections, did no good. Fortunately, however, when he began playing opposite Parker, he realized that she was a skilled and delightful actress.

The Parker role is that of a young New York actress named Sally Middleton, who is warm-hearted by nature and inclined to be in love for the sake of love. It is wartime, and eligible men are scarce, forcing Sally to select her love interests from a reduced field. Her producer (Kent Smith) stops dating her and she becomes depressed until Bill Page (Reagan), accidentally comes into her life. Page is an army sergeant in town to meet the charmingly flippant, man-loving actress Olive Lashbrook (Eve Arden). The romantically overbooked Olive has forgotten Bill, and when he encounters her, she is on a date with a naval commander (Wayne Morris), whom she passes off as her husband. Since Bill has nowhere to stay, Sally offers her apartment. It isn't long before Page develops amorous feelings for the pretty young actress. She is cautious at first, but gradually relents. By this time, Olive herself has become smitten with the soldier and is afraid of losing him to Sally. She constantly telephones the apartment and hovers near when she can, but eventually she is forced to give up and let nature take its course between Bill and Sally.

The story is slight, but Van Druten's dialogue and the deft acting by Reagan, Parker and Arden make it a genial, enjoyable picture. Reagan has never been a comic actor, but he has often revealed a sense of humor in handling comedic situations, as he does in *The Voice of the Turtle*. He says, "Comedy roles are tricky. But if they come off for me, they're the most satisfactory. Any actor, you know, will tell you that he can watch himself in a comedy part and be able to laugh at the lines and the situations. But you can't cry at yourself in a drama."

With Eleanor Parker.

JOHN LOVES MARY

A Warner Bros. Picture,
Directed by David Butler,
Produced by Jerry Wald,
Written by Phoebe and Henry Ephron, based on the
   play by Norman Krasna,
Photographed by Peverell Marley,
Music by David Buttolph,
Running time: 96 minutes.

CAST:
John Lawrence (Ronald Reagan); *Fred Taylor* (Jack Carson); *Mary McKinley* (Patricia Neal); *Lieutenant O'Leary* (Wayne Morris); *Senator McKinley* (Edward Arnold); *Lilly Herbish* (Virginia Field); *Phyllis McKinley* (Katherine Alexander); *General Biddle* (Paul Harvey); *Oscar Dugan* (Ernest Cossart); *Beachwood* (Irving Bacon); *Soldier* (George B. Hickman); *Cab driver* (Larry Rio).

With Patricia Neal and Jack Carson.

With Jack Carson.

Anyone mistaking the film *John Loves Mary* for *The Voice of the Turtle* can be excused. Ronald Reagan is again wearing the uniform of a United States Army sergeant, but this time a returning veteran, not a soldier on furlough. Reagan questioned his employers on the film: "It was great for a couple of years on Broadway but wasn't the 'returning serviceman' theme a little old hat by the time we brought it to the screen? It was." However, as with *Turtle*, Reagan was not in a strong enough position to fight the studio. If they believed that a Broadway hit about romantic misunderstandings would make it on the screen, it was fact.

Norman Krasna's play, best described as a romantic farce, opened on Broadway with William Prince as John and Nina Foch as Mary, and was an immediate success. The show was still running when Warners began filming the movie version in early 1948, which they completed in March, but did not release until January of the following year. The studio had picked the script to introduce Patricia Neal to the screen, and felt that it would serve them best to release it soon after her impressive film, *The Fountainhead.* Warners had brought the twenty-two-year-old actress to Hollywood after her success on Broadway in *Another Part of the Forest*, the Lillian Hellman play in which she played Regina—a far cry from Krasna's Mary.

With Patricia Neal and Jack Carson.

With Edward Arnold and Patricia Neal.

Mary McKinley eagerly awaits the arrival of her fiancé John Lawrence from England, where he has been serving in the army for several years. But John, it develops, owes his friend Fred (Jack Carson) a favor for saving his life in battle. Repayment concerns Fred's London girlfriend, Lilly (Virginia Field), who wants to go to the States to marry her soldier, but since she cannot go as a single girl, John marries her, intending to get a divorce when they reach America, and then marry his sweetheart, Mary. What John does not know is that Fred is already married and is an expectant father. Mary's father, Senator McKinley (Edward Arnold), arranges the marriage of his daughter to the returning soldier, but Lilly appears with her tale of woe, which creates the plot complications. An army lieutenant (Wayne Morris) unravels the problem by revealing that he had married Lilly in London and later reported himself as being killed in action to escape from the marriage; therefore, John and Lilly are not really married, leaving John to, indeed, love Mary.

John Loves Mary was briskly directed by David Butler, a veteran hand with movie light comedy, and the film pleased audiences enough to make it profitable for Warners, although not the hit they had hoped for. As Reagan points out, the subject matter was becoming passé by early 1949. It was also the kind of comedy that works well in the theatre, but thins out when examined by film cameras. Krasna admits that the play was based on a single joke—the idea of a man doing a friend a favor and getting trapped by the favor. The audience could not be allowed time to ask why the hero didn't fully explain the situation to his intended bride in the beginning. Says Reagan, ''That's exactly how the play ends, but you first have to keep the audience laughing for two hours or you have a one-reel short. We did pretty well.''

With Jack Carson and Virginia Field.

With Wayne Morris and Jack Carson.

NIGHT UNTO NIGHT

A Warner Bros. Picture,
Directed by Don Siegel,
Produced by Owen Crump,
Written by Kathryn Scola, based on the novel by
    Philip Wylie,
Photographed by Peverell Marley,

Music by Franz Waxman,
Running time: 84 minutes.

CAST:
John (Ronald Reagan); *Ann* (Viveca Lindfors);
Shawn (Broderick Crawford); *Thalia* (Rosemary

With Craig Stevens and Osa Massen.

With Osa Massen and Broderick Crawford.

DeCamp); *Gail* (Osa Massen); *Doctor Poole* (Art Baker); *Tony* (Craig Stevens); *Doctor Altheim* (Erskine Sanford); *William Shawn* (Johnny McGovern); *Willa Shawn* (Ann Burr); *Josephine* (Lillian Yarbo); *Bellboy* (Ross Ford); *Real Estate Agent* (Irving Bacon); *Maid* (Almira Sessions).

Night Unto Night was the second film made by Ronald Reagan after his return from war service, completed in January of 1947, and held back from release until June of 1949. Ironically, Warners had intended the picture as the American movie debut of Swedish actress Viveca Lindfors, but by 1949, she had left the studio. Director Don Siegel, who married Lindfors in 1949, was assigned to *Night Unto Night* because of the good results he had achieved with his first film, *The Verdict*, in 1946. He probably hoped, along with Reagan and Lindfors, that *Night Unto Night* would stay on the shelf forever, but it was not the policy of budget-minded Warners to write off a film if there was any hope of salvaging the investment. By holding the film up for two years, they counted on Lindfors being an established name with moviegoers in that time and perhaps, in conjunction with Reagan, drawing attention.

Reagan's role as an epileptic biochemist was the most difficult of his film career, but because of the scripting and conflicting viewpoints among the producers, it was impossible to make his melodramatic part credible. The role is that of a sensitive man who takes up residence in a secluded house on the Gulf Coast of Florida when he realizes his affliction is chronic. The solitude enables him to rest and to carry on with his work. His lonely beach mansion is rented from an attractive young widow

With Viveca Lindfors.

With Art Baker and Broderick Crawford.

With Viveca Lindfors.

With Viveca Lindfors.

(Lindfors). They gradually fall in love, but the biochemist cannot find the courage to tell her about his epilepsy. She also has problems; whenever she enters the rented mansion she is haunted by the voice of her late husband. The biochemist tries to convince her that the dead do not return. His own condition worsens and he has a violent fit. His physiologist (Art Baker) tells him that there is no hope. This does not dissuade the widow, who remains with the biochemist and prevents him from committing suicide during a hurricane. Love, she believes, will carry them through their troubles.

The characters lack conviction, although Reagan tries to give dignity and strength to his portrayal of the doomed biochemist, and the darkly beautiful Viveca Lindfors lends charm to her scenes. The only real merits of *Night Unto Night* are the intense musical score of Franz Waxman, the moody black-and-white photography of the veteran Peverell Mar-

ley, and the eerie atmosphere created by art director Hugh Reticker.

For an actor trying to get back into public favor, the film was a disappointing experience. Reagan admits that the Philip Wylie novel concerned unusual situations and that the film did not reap the best of it. "If you are thinking that this was a hard story to bring to life on the screen, you are right," he says. Reagan was able, however, to contribute at least one line of his own to the production. He argued with the director about the scene where the widow finds the body of her husband washed up on the beach, which causes her to go into traumatic shock and later imagine that she hears his voice. Reagan suggested to director Siegel that she might muse, "It was almost as if in death he had tried to come back to me." Says Reagan, "Frankly, I was kind of proud of it. After all, it was a basis for believing in ghosts when you stop to think he could have drifted in on any part of four thousand miles of coastline."

THE GIRL FROM JONES BEACH

A Warner Bros. Picture,
Directed by Peter Godfrey,
Produced by Alex Gottlieb,
Written by I. A. L. Diamond, based on a story by
   Allen Boretz,
Photographed by Carl Guthrie,
Music by David Buttolph,
Running time: 78 minutes.

CAST:
Bob Randolph/Robert Venerik (Ronald Reagan); *Ruth Wilson* (Virginia Mayo); *Chuck Donovan* (Eddie Bracken); *Connie Martin* (Dona Drake); *Judge John Bullfinch* (Henry Travers); *Mrs. Wilson* (Lois Wilson); *Emma Shoemaker* (Florence Bates); *Mr. Graves* (Jerome Cowan); *Miss Brooks* (Helen Westcott); *Jim Townsend* (Paul Harvey); *Mr. Ever-*

With Eddie Bracken.

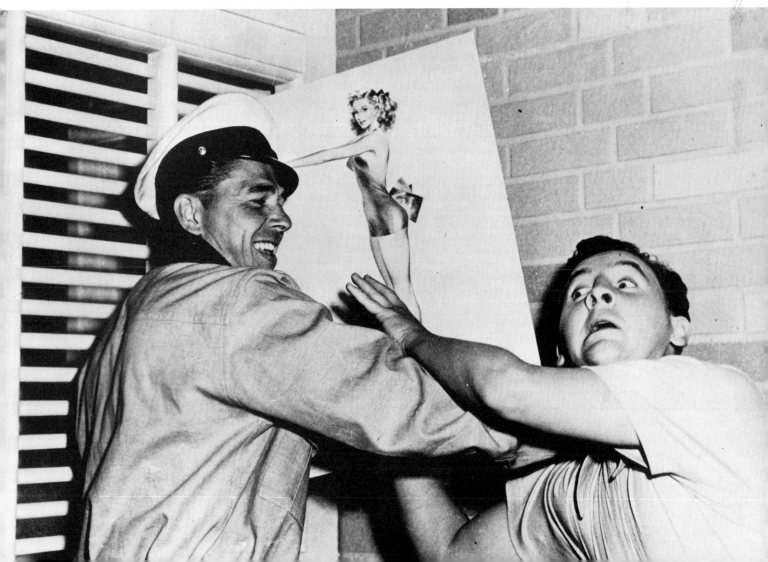

With Eddie Bracken and the twelve beauties who make up the composite of "The Randolph Girl."

With Eddie Bracken.

With Virginia Mayo.

good (Lloyd Corrigan); *Lorraine Scott* (Myrna Dell); *Mr. Woody* (William Forrest); *Woody Wilson* (Gary Gray); *Hazel* (Mary Stuart); *News Vendor* (Lennie Bremen); *Conductor* (Buddy Roosevelt).

The Girl From Jones Beach may not be a major item in Hollywood history, but it was a very profitable picture for Warners at a time when the studio was becoming concerned over the decline in box office receipts. Their films were making less money, and they lamented, along with the other studios, about what to offer the postwar public. The film was a pleasurable assignment for Ronald Reagan, and one that allowed him a wider range of expression than most of his films at that time. He was anxious to go beyond the sort of comments he received with *John Loves Mary*—that he had given a likable and thoroughly competent performance. *The Girl From Jones Beach* allowed him to indulge in some wild comedy, as well as bringing him into a gathering of attractive young actresses.

For this genial bit of cinematic fluff, Reagan plays an illustrator named Bob Randolph who wins a reputation as an artist concentrating on the ideal female form—a role clearly inspired by such contemporary painters as Vargas and Petty. He is famed for his many paintings of an ideal shape, known as "The Randolph Girl," which leads him to be approached by a television company which offers to put his gorgeous model on the air. Randolph is forced to admit that there is no single model, but that his work is a composite of a dozen girls. The company's glib publicist (Eddie Bracken) decides to seek out a beauty who resembles the ideal and use her for the program.

With Virginia Mayo.

The artist and the publicist search Jones Beach where they spot one such lovely—Ruth Wilson (Virginia Mayo), who fills out a bathing suit beautifully. She declines their offer, being a school teacher, who is more interested in improving people's minds than catering to their amorous fancies. Randolph becomes intrigued by her, and in order to get to know her better, enrolls in her citizenship class. He poses as a recent Czech immigrant, barely able to express himself in fractured English. Ruth is charmed, but soon realizes who he really is, and comes to like him despite his line of work. Trouble arises when a newspaper prints a picture of her in her glamorous bathing attire and she is upbraided by the school board. Ruth considers the members of the board stuffy invaders of her private life, and they fire her, but she takes them to court. The judge (Henry Travers) weighs the case in her favor and Ruth wins a point for the rights of women. She also wins Randolph for her husband after he resolves to employ his artistic talents along more than feminine lines.

With Lois Wilson, Gary Gray and Virginia Mayo.

165

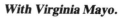

The Girl From Jones Beach is breezy escapist entertainment, with a pleasing performance from Reagan, particularly in his scenes as the phony Czech. The public had an opportunity to see a side of his talent that he formerly seldom had a chance to reveal—his sense of humor. Director Peter Godfrey did not see much humor in the script, however, and was surprised by the news that the film had broken the opening week record for the Warner Hollywood Theatre. The film has pleasant memories for Reagan, with one exception. Apparently, during a sequence involving a scene with the dozen beauties, Eddie Bracken became so enchanted with the array of pulchritude that he made Reagan trip and fall, causing him to break his coccyx.

With Dona Drake, Eddie Bracken and Virginia Mayo.

With Virginia Mayo.

166

IT'S A GREAT FEELING

A Warner Bros. Picture,
Directed by David Butler,
Produced by Alex Gottlieb,
Written by Jack Rose and Melville Shavelson, based on a story by I. A. L. Diamond,
Photographed in Technicolor by Wilfred M. Cline,
Musical direction by Ray Heindorf,
Songs by Jule Styne and Sammy Cahn,
Running time: 85 minutes.

With Wendy Lee, Jack Carson, Cosmo Sardo, Ed Agresti and Howard Washington.

With Cosmo Sardo, Ed Agresti, Jack Carson, Dennis Morgan and Howard Washington.

CAST:
Dennis Morgan and Jack Carson as themselves; *Judy Adams* (Doris Day); *Arthur Trent* (Bill Goodwin); *Clerk* (Irving Bacon); *Grace* (Claire Carleton); *Publicist* (Harlan Warde); *Secretary* (Jacqueline De Witt); *Jeffrey Bushdinkel* (Errol Flynn). *Appearing as themselves:* David Butler, Michael Curtiz, King Vidor, Raoul Walsh, Gary Cooper, Joan Crawford, Sydney Greenstreet, Danny Kaye, Patricia Neal, Eleanor Parker, Ronald Reagan, Edward G. Robinson and Jane Wyman.

It's a Great Feeling is a more valuable film today than it was when first released. Its generous views of the Warner Bros. lot and the guest appearances of a number of celebrated film folk, such as directors David Butler, King Vidor, Michael Curtiz and Raoul Walsh, and music director Ray Heindorf, combine to make the film of interest to Hollywood buffs.

The improbable story concerns Dennis Morgan and Jack Carson encountering difficulties finding a director for their upcoming picture because of Carson's inflated ego. This view of Carson is, of course, one of comic invention, and in no way relates to his actual working persona, which was agreeable and professional. But in *It's a Great Feeling*, the idea of having to work with Carson causes stars like Jane Wyman to faint. With every famous director on the lot refusing to take on the job, Carson decides to direct the picture himself, and he selects a pretty studio waitress (Doris Day) as his costar. By the end of the chaotic production, she has had enough of Hollywood and its wild characters, and returns to her small Wisconsin hometown to marry her boyfriend Jeffrey Bushdinkle, who looks like (and is!) Errol Flynn.

Reagan's appearance in the picture is a cameo bit. Jack Carson sits in a barbershop chair, wailing about his film problems to the man in the chair next to him who has his face covered. The barber pulls back the cover and it's Reagan, who wishes Jack luck.

THE HASTY HEART

A Warner Bros. Picture,
Directed by Vincent Sherman,
Produced by Howard Lindsay and Russell Crouse,
Written by Ranald MacDougall, based on the play by
   John Patrick,
Musical direction by Louis Levy,

Photographed by Wilkie Cooper,
Running time: 99 minutes.

CAST:
Lachie (Richard Todd); *Yank* (Ronald Reagan); *Sister Margaret* (Patricia Neal); *Colonel Dunn* (An-

With Patricia Neal.

With Richard Todd.

thony Nicholis); *Tommy* (Howard Crawford); *Aussie* (John Sherman); *New Zealand* (Ralph Michael); *Orderly* (Alfred Bass); *Blossom* (Orlando Martins).

Ronald Reagan approached one of his best films, *The Hasty Heart,* with mixed feelings. The role was excellent, but it required him to go to England for filming. Britain, in its postwar economy, had passed a ruling about the amount of money American producers could take out of the country. A portion of foreign profits made on British soil were to be frozen, and thus the Hollywood studios began making pictures in England, using their British bank accounts. Reagan felt this was a poor show of gratitude toward American contributions to the war effort. He also discovered the more leisurely British methods of making pictures, with "tea breaks" and strict adherence to union rulings. *The Hasty Heart* was four months in production in the latter part of 1949, which exposed Reagan to the chill and dampness of English winter weather. An English friend warned him, "You won't mind our winter outdoors —it's indoors that's really miserable." *The Hasty Heart* is set in Burma, requiring the actors to wear light tropical garb on a drafty sound stage at Elstree.

With Richard Todd.

The Ranald MacDougall screenplay is a fine treatment of the successful John Patrick play. The central character is a dour and prickly young Scottish soldier, Lachie (Richard Todd), who rebuffs the friendship offered to him by his fellow patients at a British military hospital in Burma. The most persistent in his attempts to reach the Scot is an American soldier, known to the others as Yank (Reagan), who is recovering from malaria. Their nurse is the gentle but disciplined Sister Margaret (Patricia Neal), who is particularly sympathetic toward the Scot because she knows, and he doesn't, that he is dying. Lachie comes from a hard, loveless background and his fierce independence masks his insecurity and his lack of social grace. He cannot relate to the others in the ward, all of whom are fairly happy in the knowledge that they will soon be well enough to leave Burma. The colonel (Anthony Nicholis) in charge of the hospital asks the other men to be nice to Lachie because he is a terminal case, but Lachie is a difficult case.

On the occasion of Lachie's twenty-first birthday, the patients stage a party for him and present him with a new Scottish uniform, complete with kilt. Lachie is deeply touched—more than ever before in his life—and he softens in his manners and becomes friendly toward the others. When Lachie learns from the colonel that he is a terminal case, he reverts to his former bitter, angry self and tells the men he resents their friendship, which he feels was given out of pity. He is given the choice of staying in the hospital or going home for the short time he has left to live, and Lachie decides to leave, although he knows he has no one waiting for him in Scotland. The amiable Yank explodes in anger, telling Lachie that he is lucky to have made friends who are willing to stand by him to the end. Better to die in the company of people who know and care about him than to leave and die alone. Lachie's own belief that "sorrow is born in the hasty heart" now applies to his swift rejection of their friendship. He relents and decides to spend his last few days with his friends.

The Hasty Heart met with good reviews and strong audience acceptance everywhere. Ronald Reagan was complimented for his portrayal of the compassionate but strong-minded Yank, and Patricia Neal was applauded as the vulnerable nurse. But the lion's share of the acclaim went to Richard Todd, and deservedly so. Todd was thirty years old and had been a British paratrooper during the war. The Scottish actor had stage experience, but had

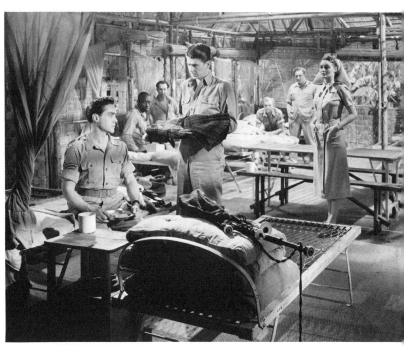

With Richard Todd.

appeared in only one prior movie, *For Them That Trespass.* His performance as Lachie won him an Academy Award nomination, but Broderick Crawford won for his portrayal in *All the King's Men.*

After completing the picture, Reagan indulged in a vacation and toured through Wales, Ireland and France. Ironically, the excellence of his work in *The Hasty Heart* did not immediately improve his stock at Warners. He had been badgering the studio for a good outdoor film, preferably a first-rate western. Just prior to leaving for England he was told that the studio had bought *Ghost Mountain* as he had requested. On returning to California he found *Ghost Mountain* had instead been set as an Errol Flynn film and retitled *Rocky Mountain.* Warner Bros. argued that Reagan had not been getting the results they expected at the box office with his pictures, particularly with *That Hagen Girl* and *Night Unto Night,* a common Hollywood tactic in controlling their stars.

Reagan's contract with Warners ran three years longer, but it was a time when the studios were hit by the impact of television and were seeking ways to get out of their contracts with even the biggest stars. Reagan's agent, Lew Wasserman, approached Warners with a compromise for a revision that would allow the actor to make one film each year for Warners at half his former annual salary, with the freedom to work at other studios as well. Warners agreed, and Reagan was permitted to branch out from the studio he had signed with in 1937. "My face was saved and the studio wasn't hurt. One week later Lew added a five-year, five-picture deal at Universal, and I bellied up to the bar like a conquering hero ordering drinks for the house. You could hardly see my wounded ego under all those $75,000 plasters."

The first project for which Universal slated Reagan was a thriller costarring Ida Lupino. But while playing in a fund-raising baseball game with fellow film celebrities, Reagan was knocked off his feet, resulting in multiple fractures to his right thigh. It was six months before he would be in condition to return to making pictures.

LOUISA

A Universal Picture,
Directed by Alexander Hall,
Produced by Robert Arthur,
Written by Stanley Roberts,
Photographed by Maury Gertsman,
Music by Frank Skinner,
Running time: 90 minutes.

CAST:
Hal Norton (Ronald Reagan); *Mr. Burnside* (Charles Coburn); *Meg Morton* (Ruth Hussey); *Mr. Hammond* (Edmund Gwenn); *Louisa Norton* (Spring Byington); *Cathy Norton* (Piper Laurie); *Jimmy Blake* (Scotty Beckett); *Gladys* (Connie Gilchrist); *Dick Stewart* (Willard Waterman); *Chris Norton* (Jimmy Hunt); *Lil Stewart* (Marjorie Crossland); *Stacy Walker* (Terry Frost); *Bob Stewart* (Martin Milner); *Miss Randall* (Ann Pearce); *Joe Collins* (Dave Willock).

Ronald Reagan's first movie for Universal was a charming and rather unusual comedy. The subject of love on the screen had long been associated with the young, causing a film titled *Louisa* to most likely concern a giddy, pretty girl. But the lady of the title is a grandmother, and the story revolves around her pursuit by a pair of elderly, but spirited swains.

In this film, Reagan appears as a genial, middle-aged architect named Hal Norton, who has a nice wife (Ruth Hussey), a pretty daughter (Piper Laurie) and a good livelihood. His problem is that his mother, Louisa (Spring Byington), arrives for a visit and soon creates tension with her cheerfully fussy ways. Her son suggests that she join a ladies' club, but in setting out to do that she runs into a local grocer, Mr. Hammond (Edmund Gwenn), who charms her with his knowledge of gourmet cooking and his amusing command of the language. They

With Ruth Hussey.

With Ruth Hussey and Spring Byington.

With Piper Laurie, Charles Coburn, Scotty Beckett and Ruth Hussey.

quarrel and then make up. As romance blossoms between the elderly pair, Hal voices his objection, thinking that the grocer is after his mother's money. Mr. Hammond is nevertheless invited to the Norton home for dinner and finds he has a rival in Hal's boss, Mr. Burnside (Charles Coburn), who is also fascinated with Louisa.

As Mr. Burnside makes inroads in his courting of Louisa, Mr. Hammond becomes more annoyed, as he wants to marry her. At a country club gathering, the two rivals play competitive games, with Mr. Burnside getting the better of Mr. Hammond at every turn. This displeases Louisa, who feels Hal's business tycoon boss is too rough on the gentle grocer, and she consoles the latter. Mr. Burnside next hires detectives to find out about Mr. Hammond's past life and comes up with the startling information that the grocer was married four times in his native England. More complications arise until Mr. Hammond explains that he loved his late wife so much that they performed a marriage ceremony every ten years and called themselves by other names each time. This romantic disclosure beguiles Louisa and she agrees to become the second Mrs. Hammond. The tycoon gallantly steps aside.

Louisa is, as Reagan says, "A good and healthy plus to any list of screen credits." His performance as the harrassed head of the family received positive notices and he regards the film fondly because of the pleasure of working with the delightful Spring Byington and the beguiling Edmund Gwenn, not to mention a reunion with his fellow actor from *Kings Row*, Charles Coburn.

With Ruth Hussey, Piper Laurie and Spring Byington.

and Marsha resolves to turn Hank in to the police. He takes her by force to a Klan meeting, where Barr decides that she should be flogged before being sent out of town, and further beaten if she talks. This violence is interrupted by Rainey's arrival with Lucy and the police. Rainey identifies many of the Klansmen, even though they are hooded. Barr tells Rainey that the death of the man dragged from jail was accidental, and that Hank fired the shot. Hank panics and shoots at Barr, hitting Lucy, and then is gunned down by a policeman. Barr is arrested, and the remaining Klansmen shamefully take their leave.

Storm Warning succeeds, both dramatically and morally, in indicting the Ku Klux Klan, and Reagan's performance as the dedicated attorney is strong and convincing. Much of the picture was shot in the small California town of Corona, which seemed to the producers to be the quintessential American community because of the town's layout. It had a court house, a library, a church, an undertaking parlor and a service station spread over four corners of a downtown intersection. Corona was also rumored at that time to be a center for California KKK activity. At one point Reagan was approached by a man who claimed to be a member and informed him that he had plenty of Klan robes to rent the production company.

Storm Warning was the first film in Reagan's new deal with Warners, one calling for him to make a picture each year over a three-year span. It was a good start, and one for which Reagan credits producer Jerry Wald. Reagan had known him since he was signed by Warners, and Wald had been a writer on several of the early Reagan pictures. Wald had become a top producer and Reagan felt confidant of a better grade of script coming his way. Unfortunately, Wald left Warners to set up his own production unit and the two men missed the opportunity to work together again.

With Raymond Greenleaf, Hugh Sanders, Dave McMahon, Richard Medina and Stuart Randall.

With Hugh Sanders.

With Sean McClory, Janet Barrett and Ginger Rogers (back to camera).

successful for them in the thirties, with their attacks on injustices in the American way of life. In 1937 they made *Black Legion* and indicted the Ku Klux Klan. *Storm Warning*, thirteen years later, suggested that little progress had been made in halting the fascistic vigilantes of the Deep South. It was a particularly interesting film for Ronald Reagan in the role of a prosecutor crusading to break up the Klan.

The focal character of the film is a New York fashion model, Marsha Mitchell (Ginger Rogers), who visits her young, newly married sister, Lucy (Doris Day), in a small southern town. Soon after arriving on a night bus, Marsha witnesses a group of hooded KKK members dragging a man from jail and killing him. Two of the men remove their hoods and Marsha sees Charlie Barr (Hugh Sanders) and the killer, Hank Rice (Steve Cochran). When she reaches her sister's home, she discovers that Hank is the husband. Lucy, being pregnant and very much in love with the boyish Hank, begs her sister to forget the incident. Marsha reluctantly agrees, but District Attorney Burt Rainey (Reagan) learns that Marsha was a witness, and subpoenas her to appear in court. Rainey is determined to wipe out the local KKK chapter, but Marsha denies being able to identify any of the men.

The Klansmen celebrate their victory and Hank gets drunk. Marsha packs to leave and Hank begins to make passes at her. When Lucy tries to intercede, Hank beats both women. The brutal behavior proves that Hank is vicious and dangerous,

With Sean McClory (right).

With Stuart Randall.

STORM WARNING

A Warner Bros. Picture,
Directed by Stuart Heisler,
Produced by Jerry Wald,
Written by Daniel Fuchs and Richard Brooks,
Photographed by Carl Guthrie,
Music by Daniele Amfitheatroff,
Running time: 93 minutes.

CAST:
Marsha Mitchell (Ginger Rogers); *Burt Rainey* (Ronald Reagan); *Lucy Rice* (Doris Day); *Hank Rice* (Steve Cochran); *Charlie Barr* (Hugh Sanders); *Cliff Rummel* (Lloyd Gough); *Faulkner* (Raymond Greenleaf); *George Athens* (Ned Glass); *Bledsoe* (Walter Baldwin); *Cora Athens* (Lynne Whitney); *Walters* (Stuart Randall); *Shore* (Sean McClory); *Hauser* (Paul Burns); *Hollis* (Dave McMahon); *Jaeger* (Robert Williams); *Wally* (Charles Watts).

In making *Storm Warning*, Warner Bros. resumed the kind of social crusading that had been so

With Stuart Randall and Ginger Rogers.

With Charles Coburn and Piper Laurie.

With Ruth Hussey, Piper Laurie and Jimmy Hunt.

*With Piper Laurie, Ruth Hussey, Scotty Beckett,
Charles Coburn, Spring Byington and Edmund Gwenn.*

BEDTIME FOR BONZO

**A Universal Picture,
Directed by Frederick de Cordova,
Produced by Michel Kraike,
Written by Val Burton and Lou Breslow, based on a
  story by Raphel David Blau and Ted Berkman,
Photographed by Carl Guthrie,
Music by Frank Skinner,
Running time: 84 minutes.**

CAST:
Peter Boyd (Ronald Reagan); *Jane* (Diana Lynn);

Professor Neumann (Walter Slezak); *Babcock* (Jesse White); *Valerie Tillinghast* (Lucille Barkley); *Dean Tillinghast* (Herbert Heyes); *Lieutenant Daggett* (Herbert Vigran); *Policeman* (Ed Gargan); *Policeman* (Howard Banks); *Fosdick* (Ed Clark); *Mr. DeWit* (Joel Franklin); *Police Chief* (Brad Browne); *Knucksy* (Harry Tyler); *Miss Swithen* (Elizabeth Flournoy); *Fireman* (Perc Launders).

Political opponents of Ronald Reagan, and those set on denigrating his career in films, often allude to

With Walter Slezak and Bonzo.

Bedtime for Bonzo as if it were typical of his output. They assume from the title that it is a mediocre comedy and that the actor had been reduced to performing with a chimpanzee. This snide attitude makes no sense because the film is amusing, and it takes skill and composure to appear on screen with an endearing animal and not seem expendable. Reagan's quietly authoritative manner in *Bedtime for Bonzo* offers a counterpoint to the animal's natural charm.

Reagan plays a professor of psychology who has a thief for a father. Partly to defend himself from libelous remarks, but mostly to impress the dean (Herbert Heyes), whose daughter (Lucille Barkley) he wants to wed, the professor sets out to prove that environment is a more important factor in life than heredity. He borrows a chimp named Bonzo from a zoology professor (Walter Slezak) and takes the animal home, where he intends to raise it as if it were human. The professor hires a nurse (Diana Lynn) to play the role of mother, and their home life is fairly normal, except for the chimp's outbursts of mischief and happy, but rough, expressions of love. The dean's daughter grows jealous, and assumes that the nurse is doing more than playing mother to the chimp. Bonzo begins to sense that his home life with his human parents is being threatened and increases his unruly behavior.

Among other things, Bonzo is fascinated with the glitter of jewelry, and his emotional frustration prompts him to steal a valuable necklace from a store. The professor is accused of having trained the chimp to steal and he is jailed. The nurse, in love with the professor and jealous of the competition, emerges from her angry withdrawal and alerts Bonzo to the trouble he has caused. Bonzo returns the jewels from the hiding place and clears the professor, who marries the nurse and provides the lovable chimp with a permanent home.

With Bonzo and Walter Slezak.

With Diana Lynn and Bonzo.

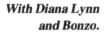

180

It is no insult to Reagan and the other humans to suggest that the film's charm rests almost entirely with its simian star. Bonzo, trained with skill, cavorts with childlike appeal. Reagan admits that the cast realized they stood small chance against such a scene stealer. "On the set he learned our business so well that going to work was a fascinating experience. Naturally his trainer was on the set, and the normal procedure called for the director, Fred de Cordova, to tell the trainer what he wanted from Bonzo. But time after time Freddie, like the rest of us, was so captivated that he'd forget and start to direct Bonzo as he did the human cast members. He'd say, 'No, Bonzo, in this scene you should . . .' Then he'd hit his head and cry, 'What the hell am I doing?'"

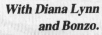

*With Diana Lynn
and Bonzo.*

THE LAST OUTPOST

A Paramount Picture,
Directed by Lewis R. Foster,
Produced by William H. Pine and William C.
   Thomas,
Written by Geoffrey Homes, George Worthing Yates
   and Winston Miller,
Photographed in Technicolor by Loyal Griggs,
Music by Lucien Cailliet,
Running time: 88 minutes.

CAST:
Vance Britten (Ronald Reagan); *Julie McCloud* (Rhonda Fleming); *Jeb Britten* (Bruce Bennett); *Sergeant Tucker* (Bill Williams); *Lieutenant Crosby* (Peter Hanson); *Calhoun* (Noah Beery, Jr.); *Lieutenant Fenton* (Hugh Beaumont); *Sam McCloud* (John Ridgely); *Mr. Delacourt* (Lloyd Corrigan); *Chief Grey Cloud* (Charles Evans).

With Hugh Beaumont, Bill Williams and Rhonda Fleming.

With Bruce Bennett.

After fourteen years in the movies, Ronald Reagan finally got to make a real western. In view of his love for horses, his life as a rancher and being an actor with a keen interest in the American West, his absence from such presents one of the ironies of life in Hollywood. The production team of William H. Pine and William C. Thomas, who had been operating their own unit at Paramount since the early forties, offered Reagan the role of a cavalry officer in a Civil War western.

The Last Outpost takes its plot line from the historical fact that the Confederacy tried to intercept gold shipments originating from the Southwest, which were bound for Union forces. The story focuses on two brothers—Vance Britten (Reagan), the officer in charge of a Confederate cavalry unit sent to Arizona to halt the supplying of gold to the

With Noah Beery, Jr.

With Bruce Bennett.

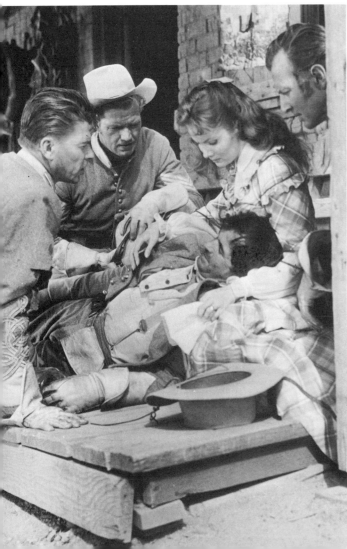

With Bill Williams, Noah Beery, Jr., Rhonda Fleming and Bruce Bennett.

With Rhonda Fleming and Lloyd Corrigan.

Northerners, and Jeb Britten (Bruce Bennett), a Union cavalry officer charged with seeing that the shipments get through. Several of the less scrupulous Unionists enlist the aid of Apaches in dispatching the Confederate interference. Vance confers with the Indians to persuade them not to become involved in the conflict. He knows that the Apaches would be a danger not only to his men, but to all the people in the Arizona Territory.

An Indian chief is shot by a renegade white, causing the dreaded Apache involvement, forcing the Confederate and Union forces to band together. Vance and his men relieve the Union garrison when it is attacked by the Indians. Vance is intent on saving the life of his ex-fiancée, Julie (Rhonda Fleming), who is at the fort with her husband (John Ridgely). When the Indians are defeated, Vance

says goodbye to his brother and returns to his home in the South.

The Last Outpost is a good western with a rugged performance from Reagan as the dashing cavalryman. It is the kind of role he could have played years earlier to place him in a better box office standing. The film became the most successful of the many Pine-Thomas entries in the adventure picture league. Throughout the forties, they had specialized in action type B movies that often starred Richard Arlen, but in the fifties, they upped their budgets to produce what might be termed A-minus pictures. Pine-Thomas never succeeded in making any notable movies, but they did manage to build up a profitable business.

The color photography of the Arizona locations and the action sequences are the main merits of *The Last Outpost*. The pleasure for Reagan in making a western was heightened when the producers permitted him to ride his own horse, Tarbaby, and shipped it to Arizona at the company's expense. Reagan states that a few cowboy extras, dressed as soldiers, were dubious about Tarbaby's stamina in the Arizona heat and the requirements of the prolonged action shooting. ''Those boys just didn't know that a thoroughbred can do anything better than any other horse, except quit. By sundown there were picture horses scattered all over the cactus patch, so beat we had trouble mustering enough for background in the close shots. But old Tarbaby was not only picture-acting—she was kicking those beat critters out of the way. 'Twas a proud moment for her owner.''

With Noah Beery, Jr., and Charles Evans.

HONG KONG

A Paramount Picture,
Directed by Lewis R. Foster,
Produced by William H. Pine and William C.
Thomas,
Written by Winston Miller, based on a story by Lewis
R. Foster,
Photographed in Technicolor by Lionel Lindon,

Music by Lucien Cailliet,
Running time: 92 minutes.

CAST:

Jeff Williams (Ronald Reagan); *Victoria Evans* (Rhonda Fleming); *Mr. Lighton* (Nigel Bruce); *Mrs. Lighton* (Lady May Lawton); *Tao Liang* (Marvin

With Danny Chang.

With Rhonda Fleming.

Miller); *Hotel Clerk* (Claude Allister); *Wei Lin* (Danny Chang).

If Ronald Reagan felt that he stood little chance of commanding screen attention opposite an ingratiating chimp in *Bedtime for Bonzo*, he must have realized a similar challenge playing with a particularly beguiling four-year-old Chinese boy in *Hong Kong*. This was his second adventure picture for Pine-Thomas at Paramount, and Reagan plays a down-at-heels ex-American soldier who stays on in the Orient after World War II, hoping to make a killing in the surplus equipment business.

Jeff Williams (Reagan) is a hard and selfish man who has become bitter about his bad luck. He fails in his business plans and gets involved in a Communist raid on China. In making his escape, he meets a

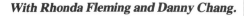

With Rhonda Fleming and Danny Chang.

With Rhonda Fleming and Danny Chang.

187

With Danny Chang.

young lad (Danny Chang), who is lost and alone. The American carries him away and the two stumble into a mission run by an American Red Cross worker, Victoria (Rhonda Fleming), who has chartered a plane to Hong Kong. She takes them with her, but soon after landing, they discover it is impossible to get hotel accommodations and in desperation they take someone else's reservation. The hard-boiled ex-soldier is exposed to the charm and innocence of the child, and the compassion of the beautiful Victoria, and finds his bitterness toward life and people lessening. But he still has a touch of larceny, and knows that the ancient Chinese idol that belongs to the boy is of value. Jeff approaches an art dealer (Marvin Miller) to sell it and eventually discovers that the dealer is in league with gang of crooks. He begins to doubt his right to steal the idol from the boy, but the crooks kidnap the child. Jeff makes a deal with them, which goes wrong, and they are all saved only by the arrival of the British police of Hong Kong. Jeff opts to settle for a decent life—to marry Victoria and pay regular visits to the orphanage in which they place the child.

Hong Kong benefits from its Technicolor photography of the teeming city streets and the nearby ricefields. For Reagan it allowed more range than usual in the depiction of character. The reviewer

With Rhonda Fleming.

With Rhonda Fleming and Marvin Miller.

for *The Hollywood Reporter* said, "Reagan's persuasive playing of the hero contributes much toward making *Hong Kong* convincing."

According to Reagan, the child actor Danny Chang was the finest and most natural scene-stealer he had met during his career. The boy's quiet manner and innocent face made him the natural point of attention. Whenever he became tired, or confused by the director, Lewis Foster, Danny would take an eternity to drink a glass of water. On one occasion, presumably when he could imbibe no more water, he simply closed his eyes and refused to open them. The director was at a loss until someone with a knowledge of child psychology suggested that they ignore Danny and play out the scene with his double. This made the child open his eyes and return to the game of acting.

SHE'S WORKING HER WAY THROUGH COLLEGE

A Warner Bros. Picture,
Directed by H. Bruce Humberstone,
Produced by William Jacobs,
Written by Peter Milne, based on the play *The Male
    Animal* by James Thurber and Elliott Nugent,
Photographed in Technicolor by Wilfred M. Cline,
Musical direction by Ray Heindorf,
Songs by Sammy Cahn and Vernon Duke,
Running time: 101 minutes.

CAST:

Angela Gardner (Virginia Mayo); *John Palmer* (Ronald Reagan); *Don Weston* (Gene Nelson); *Shep Slade* (Don DeFore); *Helen Palmer* (Phyllis Thaxter); *Ivy Williams* (Patrice Wymore); *Fred Copeland* (Roland Winters); *Dean Rogers* (Raymond Greenleaf); *Tiny Gordon* (Norman Bartold); *Maybelle* (Amanda Randolph); *Mrs. Copeland* (Henrietta Taylor); *Mrs. Rogers* (Hope Sansbury); *Professor* (George Meander); *Secretary* (Eve Miller).

Many of the Warner Bros. musicals of the 1950s were remakes of their 1930s musicals, or, in some cases, musical versions of comedies of former times. *She's Working Her Way Through College* belongs in the latter category, being a reworking of *The Male Animal* (1942) and fleshed out with a string of both new and old songs. The play, by James Thurber and Elliott Nugent, had made an excellent movie vehicle for Henry Fonda, who played a gentle, intellectual college professor who finally asserts himself amid all the rah-rah sports types who loudly dominate academe.

Much of the sociological substance of the original

With Virginia Mayo.

play was dropped for the film version. In the original, the professor had been a liberal with a passion for tolerance and the understanding of differing political viewpoints. A small amount of that stance was retained for *She's Working Her Way Through College*, the title of which refers to a burlesque queen, Angela Gardner (Virginia Mayo), who decides to give up the stage and become a writer. She enrolls in a Midwestern college and studies writing in the class of a mild-mannered professor, John Palmer (Reagan), who also directs the annual school plays. Angela becomes a boarder in the home of the professor.

Problems arise when Angela tries to persuade the professor to do a musical instead of the usual classic play for the next school production. Campus football star Don Weston (Gene Nelson) becomes enamoured of Angela, and takes a part in the musical she has written. His dancer girl-friend, Ivy (Patrice Wymore), jealously reveals Angela's burlesque background to the school board and the pompous chairman of the board (Roland Winters) demands that Palmer expel Angela from his class.

With Gene Nelson and Virginia Mayo.

With Gene Nelson, Virginia Mayo and Phyllis Thaxter.

With Phyllis Thaxter and Don DeFore.

The professor, depressed by his home life, wrongly believes his wife has become romantically reunited with a former suitor, the boastful ex-champion footballer Shep Slade (Don DeFore). Palmer refuses to expel his glamorous coed and addresses the student body on the theme of academic freedom, which makes him a campus hero. The stuffy indignation of the board chairman is quickly deflated when Angela recognizes him as a stage door Johnny who had once tried to entice her with a mink coat. The show is a hit and Angela continues her education.

Although possessing little of the intellectual and sentimental impact of *The Male Animal,* the musical version is diverting entertainment, which manages to retain the original's plea for academic rights, while parading several pleasing but unmemorable song-and-dance routines. Ronald Reagan appears to advantage as the mild-mannered professor, and he is especially good in a protracted drunken sequence played by Fonda in the previous film. Regan admits that the picture was really a showcase for the musical abilities of the delightful Virginia Mayo, who was soon rewarded with the sequel, *She's Back on Broadway,* costarring Gene Nelson.

With Virginia Mayo.

THE WINNING TEAM

A Warner Bros. Picture,
Directed by Lewis Seiler,
Produced by Bryan Foyp
Written by Ted Sherdeman, Seeleg Lester and
 Mervin Gerrard,
Photographed by Sid Hickox,
Music by David Buttolph,
Running time: 98 minutes.

CAST:
Aimee Alexander (Doris Day); *Grover C. Alexander*
(Ronald Reagan); *Hornsby* (Frank Lovejoy); *Margaret* (Eve Miller); *Bill Killefer* (James Millican);
Willie Alexander (Russ Tamblyn); *Glasheen*
(Gordon Jones); *McCarthy* (Hugh Sanders); *Sam
Arrants* (Frank Ferguson); *Pa Alexander* (Walter
Baldwin); *Ma Alexander* (Dorothy Adams); *Sister*
(Bonnie Kay Eddy); *Fred* (James Dodd); *Foreman*
(Tom Greenway); *Umpire* (Russ Clark).

The Winning Team was Ronald Reagan's final
movie for Warner Bros. He had been with the studio by that time for fifteen years and had appeared
in forty of their productions. He had been growing
ever more restless with the assignments and the
frustration of not getting the roles he wanted. The
last film for Warner Bros. was exactly his type, and
one which he claims he enjoyed almost as much as
playing George Gipp in *Knute Rockne—All American*. He portrays Grover Cleveland Alexander, one
of the foremost figures in American baseball. He
was known as Alex the Great in the first quarter of
this century, and is still discussed with awe for staging what sports historians call the greatest of all
comebacks.

The film is a reasonably accurate account of Alexander's career, except for a whitewashing of his
alcohol problem and a refusal of Warners to allow

With Doris Day.

194

With Doris Day.

any mention of his epilepsy. Alexander's widow, Aimee (played on screen by Doris Day), was hired as the story consultant and provided the writers with valuable insight into the personality and habits of her husband. Arnold "Jigger" Statz, the so-called Iron Man of the '20s, and Jerry Priddy, then the second baseman for the Detroit Tigers, were hired as technical advisors. Reagan spent two hours a day for three weeks prior to filming with Priddy, perfecting his pitching and "learning the difference between throwing from the mound and just throwing."

The film begins with Alexander's early days as a telephone lineman in Nebraska and his first successes in Midwest bush-league baseball in 1908. Within three years, his incredible skill as a pitcher elevates him to stardom with the Philadelphia Phillies. During his first year with them, he helps the team achieve twenty-eight victories. His luck starts to sour when he receives a blow on the head, which results in dizzy spells. During the First World War, he serves with the artillery and is exposed to thunderous battlefield noise, worsening his condition. Alexander becomes plagued by periods of double vision, and begins drinking to alleviate his pain. His drinking increases, and his career in baseball declines. He is dismissed from the major leagues, and takes whatever jobs he can get with semi-pro teams, but his seizures are mistaken for drunkenness and eventually Alexander leaves baseball. He thereafter takes a job as a sideshow attraction in a sleazy circus. His wife stands by him, and with the aid of his faithful friend, pitcher Bill Killifer (James Millican), she persuades the renowned baseball manager Rogers Hornsby (Frank Lovejoy) to give Alexander another chance in the major leagues.

As *The Winning Team* triumphantly reveals, Grover Cleveland Alexander did indeed get another chance. In 1926, he became the toast of baseball when he pitched for the St. Louis Cardinals against the New York Yankees at Yankee Stadium. Alexander saved the World Series and made history by pitching against such legendary players as Babe Ruth, Lou Gehrig and Lou Lazzeri. In his final play he spun his team to victory with all the bases loaded.

For baseball buffs *The Winning Team* is a favorite. The film gave Reagan one of his best opportunities as an actor, and one in which he conveyed both his own enthusiasm for the game and the glorious ups and painful downs of Grover Cleveland Alexander. It is an intelligent, skillful, sympathetic per-

195

formance. Reagan was reunited with Bryan Foy, who had produced most of the actor's early B's at Warner Bros., and who finally became a producer in the major league. Sadly, when Reagan and Foy finally made a movie together of which they were both proud, it was also their last.

During the years of his fame, Alexander hid his epilepsy from the public, preferring to be known as a drunk rather than someone suffering from a pitiable affliction. Warners took a similar tack in the film, although Reagan felt it was a mistake for the studio to foster the superstitious attitude toward epilepsy. "I've always regretted that the studio insisted we not use the word, although we tried to get the idea across. The trouble was that a frank naming of the illness would have the ring of truth, whereas ducking it made some critics accuse us of inventing something to whitewash his alcoholism. One thing we didn't invent was the love story between Alex and Aimee. He once pitched (and won) both games of a double-header so he could get a day off to be with his bride."

With *The Winning Team*, Ronald Reagan left Warners on a high, although he found it painful to leave a place of employment after so many years and so many associations. But, like all of the famous veteran stars of Warner Bros., Reagan found himself arguing more and more with Jack L. Warner, and eventually discovered those arguments to be signposts to the exit.

With Doris Day, Dorothy Adams and Kenneth Patterson.

With Doris Day.

197

Vith Frank Lovejoy.

TROPIC ZONE

A Paramount Picture,
Directed by Lewis R. Foster,
Produced by William H. Pine and William C.
  Thomas,
Written by Lewis R. Foster, based on a story by Tom
  Gill,
Photographed in Technicolor by Lionel Lindon,
Music by Lucien Cailliet,
Running time: 94 minutes.

CAST:
Dan McCloud (Ronald Reagan); *Flanders White* (Rhonda Fleming); *Elena* (Estelita); *Tapachula Sam* (Noah Beery, Jr.); *Bert Nelson* (Grant Withers); *Lukats* (John Wengraf); *Tia Feliciana* (Argentina Brunetti); *Captain Basilio* (Rico Alanez); *Marcario* (Maurice Jara); *Victoriana* (Pilar Del Rey).

With Rhonda Fleming.

Free of Warner Bros., and on his own as a free-lance actor, Ronald Reagan was faced with the problem of getting work and finding decent pictures that would maintain his star standing in the industry. He discovered, as did other actors divested of studio security, that the going was tougher than he had imagined. *Tropic Zone* was not a good portent of the future of his career.

In their search for subject matter in the adventure *genre*, William H. Pine and William C. Thomas had covered most situations in which brave and enterprising men can engage themselves. In *Tropic Zone*, Pine-Thomas explored the hazards of growing bananas amid greed and corruption in Central America. The film is actually a western, with plantations instead of ranches, and bananas instead of cattle.

Into this humid milieu comes Dan McCloud (Reagan), a rougish American on the run from a neighboring republic because of his involvement in a deposed political faction. Since McCloud is an expert fruit farmer, he is given a job by the local banana baron (John Wengraf), who controls much of the

With Rhonda Fleming and John Wengraf.

With Rhonda Fleming.

With Grant Withers.

state of Puerto Barrancas, including the services of the chief of police (Rico Alanez). The greedy baron wants to take over all of the plantations, one of which is owned by lovely Flanders White (Rhonda Fleming), who resists selling. The charming baron appoints McCloud her foreman, although his real object is to bring on ruin. With Flanders out of the way, the few remaining independent growers would fall to the doublecrossing baron, who owns the only export ship in the country. But he doesn't count on the basic decency of McCloud, who falls in love with the gorgeous Flanders and secretly plots against the baron. McCloud unites all the independent growers and gradually builds his plans to the day of revolution. With the despot overthrown, McCloud settles down happily with the leading lady.

Paramount invested *Tropic Zone* with some good action sequences, and the expert use of Technicolor gives life to otherwise lackluster footage. The film shows how bananas are grown and harvested, but as Reagan says, "I knew the script was hopeless, but there was a little matter of a debt of gratitude because they had given me *The Last Outpost* when no one else would let me get outdoors." Reagan's performance in *Tropic Zone* is pleasing, and not difficult for a veteran.

200

With Estelita and Noah Beery, Jr.

201

With Rhonda Fleming.

LAW AND ORDER

A Universal Picture,
Directed by Nathan Juran,
Produced by John W. Rogers,
Written by John and Owen Bagni and D. D.
Beauchamp, based on a story by William R.
Burnett,
Photographed in Technicolor by Clifford Stine,
Music by Joseph Gershenson,
Running time: 80 minutes.

CAST:
Frame Johnson (Ronald Reagan); *Jeannie Bristow* (Dorothy Malone); *Lute Johnson* (Alex Nicol); *Kurt Durning* (Preston Foster); *Maria* (Ruth Hampton); *Jimmy Johnson* (Russell Johnson); *Fin Elder* (Barry Kelley); *Denver Cahoon* (Chubby Johnson); *Frank Durling* (Dennis Weaver); *Jed* (Jack Kelly); *Clarissa* (Valerie Jackson); *Johnny Benton* (Don Garner); *Dixon* (Tom Browne); *Judge Williams* (Richard

Ronald Reagan's persistent desire to make westerns came to fruition in the later years of his film career, although somewhat too late to affect the course of that history. He readily accepted Universal's offer to star in *Law and Order* because of the role of a gunslinging lawman, which tied in with his love of Americana and his feeling that westerns were a form of entertainment understandable by all moviegoers. Stories about the Wild West were, he felt, "recent enough to be real and old enough to be romantic. Mix that up with horses, action, a little love, and lots of money and you've found a rich strike."

Law and Order is hardly a rich strike, but it may be considered a solid, conventional western of the "retired gunfighter" breed. Frame Johnson (Reagan) is a respected lawman who has cleaned up the wicked ways of Tombstone, Arizona, and wants to retire to the life of a rancher. This pleases his fiancée, Jeannie (Dorothy Malone), who runs the saloon left to her by her father. She, too, is eager to leave the rough community and be her beau's wife. With his brothers, Lute (Alex Nicol) and Jimmy (Russell Johnson), and their undertaker friend, Denver (Chubby Johnson), Frame proceeds to the town of Cottonwood. Unfortunately, Cottonwood is under the domination of Kurt Durning (Preston Foster), who hates Frame because he crippled him in a previous encounter.

The citizens of Cottonwood appeal to the famous marshal to take up the badge of law and order once again and rid them of Durning. Frame declines, but Lute accepts, which soon costs him his life when he tries to apprehend one of Durning's sons. Frame takes the job as marshal and brings the Durning

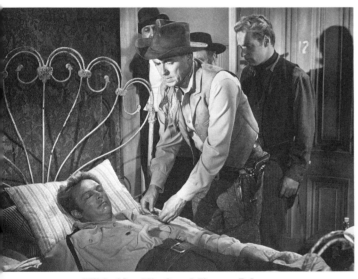

With Alex Nicol and Jimmy Johnson.

With Jimmy Johnson.

203

With Alex Nicol.

With Jimmy Johnson and Alex Nicol.

With Preston Foster.

204

With Dorothy Malone.

empire to an end. This also requires him by law to arrest his brother Jimmy for killing another Durning, although in self-defense. Jimmy flees, but Frame goes after him, proving that the law applies to everyone, and that it must be enforced. With Cottonwood back in honest hands, Frame and his bride settle down to ranch life.

Law and Order would probably have been a good B western in the thirties, starring Buck Jones or Ken Maynard, but by the early fifties, such stale fare was relegated to celluloid history. Universal pumped this film with production values, making it only a modest A picture. As such, it was a firm investment for the studio, and an enjoyable vehicle for western buffs and horse-lover Ronald Reagan.

With Dorothy Malone.

PRISONER OF WAR

An MGM Picture,
Directed by Andrew Marton,
Produced by Henry Berman,
Written by Allen Rivkin,
Photographed by Robert Planck,
Music by Jeff Alexander,
Running time: 80 minutes.

CAST:
Web Sloane (Ronald Reagan); *Joseph Robert Stanton* (Steve Forrest); *Jesse Treadman* (Dewey Martin); *Colonel Biroshilov* (Oscar Homolka); *Francis Belney* (Robert Horton); *Captain Jack Hodges* (Paul Stewart); *Major O. D. Halle* (Harry Morgan); *Lieutenant Robovnik* (Stephen Bekassy); *Colonel Kim*

With Henry Morgan.

Doo Yi (Leonard Strong); *Merton Tolliver* (Darryl Hickman).

After turning down scripts for a half year because they were either too feeble, or totally uninteresting, Ronald Reagan received one he immediately accepted. Just before Christmas, 1953, MGM sent him *Prisoner of War,* a story of the mistreatment and brainwashing of American captives during the Korean War. The facts of captivity were verified in conversations with the officer assigned as technical adviser to the film, who had been imprisoned in North Korea and lost ninety pounds while in captivity.

Writer Allen Rivkin had based his script on many true stories from ex-prisoners. Rivkin interviewed dozens of men and learned of the prolonged hardships of the severe Korean winters, the lack of food and medical supplies, and attempts by the Koreans to politically alter the thoughts of the American ser-

With Dewey Martin.

With Oscar Homolka, Stephen Bekassy and Dewey Martin.

With Steve Forrest and Dewey Martin.

vicemen. Rivkin heard of men who arrogantly defied the Koreans, others who pretended to be impressed in order to get better treatment, and those who cracked under torture and cooperated. Some servicemen seemed genuinely impressed with the Communist cause, and said so on their return to America. Such is the substance of *Prisoner of War*, which MGM produced as quickly as possible in order to get the film into the theatres while the news of returning prisoners was still fresh in the public mind.

Reagan plays an army officer named Web Sloane, who volunteers to find out about the rumors of brutality in the Korean prisoner camps. He parachutes behind the lines and sneaks into a group of Americans being marched to such a camp. There he sees every kind of torture and beating, and he also undergoes savage treatment, as well as being forced to attend lectures of indoctrination given by Korean officials. A Russian colonel (Oscar Homolka) directs the vicious brainwashing sessions. Among the prisoners are a soldier (Steve Forrest) who defies his captors at every turn, resulting in beatings, and another (Dewey Martin), who seemingly knuckles under to the processing in order to get medical drugs for a suffering fellow prisoner. Sloane discovers that everything he feared about the brutal Korean treatment is true.

Prisoner of War made only a modest impact on critics and a public already saturated with news of the Korean War camps. Says Reagan, "The picture should have done better. Every torture scene and incident was based on actual happenings documented in official army records. Unfortunately, production and release were both rushed, with the idea the picture should come out while the headlines were hot." He adds that it is a story deserving of a more comprehensive treatment.

With Steve Forrest.

With Oscar Homolka, Dewey Martin and Stephen Bekassy.

On the set with technical adviser Capt. Robert H. Wise and writer Allen Rivkin.

CATTLE QUEEN OF MONTANA

An RKO Picture,
Directed by Allan Dwan,
Produced by Benedict Borgeaus,
Written by Robert Blees and Howard Estabrook,
    based on a story by Thomas Blackburn,
Photographed in Technicolor by John Alton,
Music by Louis Forbes,
Running time: 88 minutes.

CAST:

Sierra Nevada Jones (Barbara Stanwyck); *Farrell* (Ronald Reagan); *Tom McCord* (Gene Evans); *Colorados* (Lance Fuller); *Nachakos* (Anthony Caruso); *Yost* (Jack Elam); *Starfire* (Yvette Dugay); *Pop Jones* (Morris Ankrum); *Nat* (Chubby Johnson); *Hank* (Myron Healey); *Powhani* (Rod Redwing); *Colonel Carrington* (Paul Birch); *Land Office Clerk* (Byron Foulger); *Dan* (Burt Mustin).

With Barbara Stanwyck.

With Hugh Sanders.

Ronald Reagan was pleased to accept the lead in another western and delighted that it would be shot in Technicolor in Glacier National Park, Montana, an area of the country new to him. The location setting was a wise selection on the part of producer Benedict Borgeaus, since the scenery is perhaps the best thing about *Cattle Queen of Montana,* an otherwise conventional western saga.

The title applies to a lady known as Sierra Nevada Jones (Barbara Stanwyck), who, despite the name, is from Texas. She and her rancher father (Morris Ankrum) arrive in Montana, having driven their vast herd of cattle up from the Lone Star State in order to settle in the verdant mountain meadows of the Northwest. Their plans are soon shattered when they are raided by Indians, who drive off their cattle and kill the old man. The Indians are actually in the employ of a local outlaw, Tom McCord (Gene Evans), who plans to build a cattle empire. As the plot develops, a man named Farrell (Reagan) comes on the scene. He is an undercover army officer sent by Washington to investigate the Indian disturbances and the rustling reports. Farrell's efforts end McCord's plans and soothe the restless Indians,

211

and naturally, he falls in love with and weds Sierra Nevada Jones. The heroine thus retrieves her cattle, and she and Farrell run the ranch together.

John Alton's fine color photography of the spectacular mountains and landscapes, plus the visually exciting sequence of the Indians stampeding the cattle herd, lift *Cattle Queen of Montana* above the average western. Another story element concerns the Blackfeet Indians. The plot gives some insight into social conflicts within the tribe, as a university-educated brave (Lance Fuller) gains control over the ruinous leadership of a greedy type (Anthony Caruso), who is in league with the villainous McCord.

Reagan's role as the hero was a chance to play tourist at company expense. "Somehow working

With Barbara Stanwyck.

With Lance Fuller and Anthony Caruso.

outdoors amid beautiful scenery and much of the time on horseback never has seemed like work to me. It's like getting paid for playing cowboy and Indian.'' Also a pleasure for Reagan was the opportunity to play opposite Barbara Stanwyck, an actress with a notable reputation for being easy to work with and for always being civilized toward the crews of her pictures. According to Reagan, she did most of her own stunts in the film, including bathing in an ice cold lake. Stanwyck's impression on the Blackfeet Indians was so positive that she was made a blood sister of the tribe and given the title Princess Many Victories. Whenever they have met since then, Reagan calls her by her Indian name.

With Rod Redwing and Barbara Stanwyck.

With Barbara Stanwyck.

TENNESSEE'S PARTNER

An RKO Picture,
Directed by Allan Dwan,
Produced by Benedict Borgeaus,
Written by Milton Krims, D. D. Beauchamp,
  Graham Baker and Teddi Sherman, based on a
  story by Bret Harte,
Photographed in Eastman Color by John Alton,
Music by Louis Forbes,
Running time: 86 minutes.

CAST:

Tennessee (John Payne); *Elizabeth Farnham* (Rhonda Fleming); *Cowpoke* (Ronald Reagan); *Goldie* (Coleen Gray); *Turner* (Anthony Caruso); *Sheriff* (Leo Gordon); *Reynolds* (Myron Healey); *Judge* (Morris Ankrum); *Grubstake McNiven* (Chubby Johnson); *Prendergast* (Joe Devlin); *Clifford* (John Mansfield); *Girl* (Angie Dickinson).

Producer Benedict Borgeaus retained Ronald Reagan's services for a follow-up to *Cattle Queen of Montana*, and brought back veteran director Allen Dwan and photographer John Alton. Reagan was again in the saddle, this time in a California mining camp setting. The screenplay was based on a Bret Harte frontier adventure yarn, but was so changed that Harte would have had difficulty recognizing the story. Harte had traveled to California in 1854 to capture some of the excitement of the gold rush, and over the years he wrote the stories that have made him famous. *Tennessee's Partner,* as written by Harte, concerns an unscrupulous rogue known as Tennessee, who takes off with his partner's wife and commits highway robbery. His partner, Cowpoke, remains loyal and even tries to bribe the jury at his trial, but to no avail; Tennessee is hanged.

In the Borgeaus version, Tennessee (John Payne) is a slick gambler in the raucous mining town of Sandy Bar, where his lady friend, Elizabeth

(Rhonda Fleming), runs a glorified saloon called "The Marriage Market." Tennessee rakes in a good income under these auspices and any gambler who questions his honesty risks being killed because Tennessee is a fast gun. At one point, a disgruntled prospector is about to cancel Tennessee's skills when the hard-hitting Cowpoke (Reagan) arrives in the saloon and saves Tennessee. The men become quick friends.

Cowpoke has come to Sandy Bar to marry his girl friend Goldie (Coleen Gray), a gold digger in the worst sense and, in the opinion of Tennessee, a scheming trollop. In order to save Cowpoke from being fleeced by Goldie, Tennessee woos her, to the consternation of his friend. Despite the conflict between them, Cowpoke comes to Tennessee's defense when he is again in danger of being killed by a claim jumper (Anthony Caruso), who is trying to frame Tennessee for the murder of a popular prospector (Chubby Johnson). Saving Tennessee's life costs Cowpoke his own, when he is gunned down in the fight. The grateful friend gives Cowpoke a fine funeral and marries Elizabeth, who understands the ruse to save Cowpoke from Goldie.

With Morris Ankrum, John Payne and Leo Gordon.

With Coleen Gray and Rhonda Fleming.

Tennessee's Partner deserves an honorable mention as an offbeat item set in a California mining town. The film captures the lusty atmosphere of the era, with rampant gold fever, excitement, violence and shifty characters. Allan Dwan (seventy years of age at the time of filming) can be credited for the success of this western. Dwan had started his Hollywood career in 1911, and showed an early marked talent for directing fast-paced adventure films, such as Douglas Fairbanks' *The Iron Mask* (1929), Randolph Scott's *Frontier Marshal* (1939) and John Wayne's *Sands of Iwo Jima* (1949).

The film is a good showcase for Ronald Reagan, as the tough, heart-of-gold Cowpoke, but it is really a supporting role to John Payne's brash frontier cad, a performance on Payne's part that may be considered his best in a long and rather undistinguished movie career.

Reagan was less interested in his Hollywood progress, as by this time, he was becoming engaged in television. Two years would pass before he would appear again on movie theatre screens.

With Rhonda Fleming and John Payne.

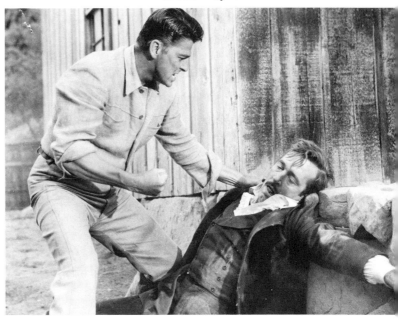

With John Payne.

217

HELLCATS OF THE NAVY

A Columbia Picture,
Directed by Nathan Juran,
Produced by Charles H. Schneer,
Written by David Lang and Raymond Marcus, based
**   on the book by Charles A. Lockwood and Hans**
**   Christian Adamson,**
Photographed by Irving Lippman,
Music by Mischa Bakaleinikoff,
Running time: 81 minutes.

CAST:
Commander Casey Abbott (Ronald Reagan); *Helen Blair* (Nancy Davis); *Lieutenant Commander Don Landon* (Arthur Franz); *Freddy Warren* (Robert Arthur); *Lieutenant Paul Prentice* (William Leslie); *Carroll* (William Phillips); *Wes Barton* (Harry Lauter); *Charlie* (Michael Garth); *Chick* (Joseph Turkel); *Jug* (Don Keefer); *Admiral Nimitz* (Selmer Jackson); *Admiral Lockwood* (Maurice Manson).

With Arthur Franz and Bing Russell.

With Maurice Manson (as Admiral Lockwood) and Selmer Jackson (as Admiral Nimitz).

With Arthur Franz.

Based on the book by Admirals Charles A. Lockwood and Hans Christian Adamson, *Hellcats of the Navy* deals with an actual naval operation against the Japanese. Fleet Admiral Chester W. Nimitz introduces the picture, since Nimitz himself was the supervisor of the 1944 campaign in the Tsushima Strait and the Sea of Japan to get American submarines through the enemy minefields. (The Nimitz character in the film is played by Selmer Jackson.) It was Ronald Reagan's premiere on the screen as a naval officer, and his first and only film with his second wife, Nancy Davis (in the role of a navy nurse).

The "hellcats" of the title are a branch of the submarine service charged with unusual operations. They are to bring back sample Japanese mines from enemy waters in order that United States Navy experts can learn why the mines are resistant to sonar detection. Once this obstacle has been eliminated, the Navy will be able to approach Japanese shipping routes. The man assigned to this mission is Commander Casey Abbott (Reagan), who succeeds in penetrating the mined straits with his submarine, the *Starfish*. He is forced to abandon one of his frogmen, Barton (Harry Lauter), when an enemy warship bears down on the submarine. This action incurs the resentment of his second in command, Landon (Arthur Franz), who feels that the captain may have had an ulterior motive. Barton was known to have made advances to the skipper's girlfriend, Helen (Nancy Davis).

Landon's bitterness is increased when Abbott lists him in his report as being a good junior officer, although emotionally unsuitable for command. Back at base, Helen assures Abbott that her friendship for the late frogman was not serious and was in fact caused by Abbott's own refusal to marry her until the war was over. The *Starfish* is sent back into the Tsushima Strait once the naval experts have solved the sonar problems and is instructed to clear the minefields and proceed with the attack. After several encounters with the enemy, Abbott devises a scheme to map a course through the minefields. He is successful in following a Japanese vessel and charting a course, but loses his damaged submarine when it is forced to surface. He and a handful of his men, including Landon, survive the action and are picked up by a United States Navy flying boat. Later Abbott leads a flotilla of submarines through the strait and wreaks havoc on enemy shipping.

En route back to the base, Abbott's new subma-

rine develops problems when wires entangle the rudder. Abbott climbs into a diving suit to rectify the problem, but a Japanese destroyer approaches and Landon gives the order to submerge. Landon engages and sinks the enemy, and then searches for his commanding officer, who is found, injured but alive. On his recovery Abbott submits another report on Landon, this one commending him for bravery and recommending him for a command of his own. He also decides to marry Helen.

While dealing with an interesting segment of Second World War naval operations, *Hellcats of the Navy* seems an odd choice of material for 1957 release. It is the kind of film Warner Bros. made during wartime—and much better. Ronald Reagan should have been put to use at that time.

With Nancy Davis.

221

THE KILLERS

AN NBC-TV Picture,
Directed and produced by Don Siegel,
Written by Gene L. Coon, based on the story by
** Ernest Hemingway,**
Photographed in color by Richard L. Rawlings,
Music by John Williams,
Running time: 95 minutes.

CAST:
Charlie Strom (Lee Marvin); *Johnny North* (John Cassavetes); *Sheila Farr* (Angie Dickinson); *Browning* (Ronald Reagan); *Lee* (Clu Gulager); *Earl Sylvester* (Claude Akins); *Mickey* (Norman Fell); *Miss Watson* (Virginia Christine); *Mail truck driver* (Don Haggerty); *George* (Robert Phillips); *Recep-*

tionist (Kathleen O'Malley); *Gym assistant* (Ted Jacques); *Guard* (Irving Mosley); *Salesman* (Jimmy Joyce); *Desk clerk* (Scott Hale); *Clerk* (Seymour Cassel).

Hellcats of the Navy would have been Ronald Reagan's last feature film if his next picture, *The Killers*, made for television, had not been considered too violent for the home screen. *The Killers* is the least typical of all his films, and the only one to present him as a thoroughly mean and unpleasant character.

In 1946 Universal produced *The Killers* in a screenplay by Anthony Veiller. It was an imaginative expansion of a short story by Ernest Hemingway which briefly tells of two men waiting in a diner for a man they have been hired to kill. The man is aware of them, but too world-weary to care. The

With John Cassavetes, Robert Phillips, Norman Fell and Angie Dickinson.

With Angie Dickinson.

223

Hemingway story is an exercise in fatalism. No reason is given for the man being marked for death. Veiller's treatment did speculate on the possible reasons, and Burt Lancaster (in his introductory film) was cast as the man resigned to die. *The Killers* was an impressive and successful venture, but the 1964 version offers a new approach by Gene L. Coon and is much less powerful.

In 1963, Universal, and their subsidiary, Revue Productions, devised a series called *Project 120,* to churn out feature films of good quality for television and release them as theatre products. The concept was prompted by the dwindling number of features being made in the early sixties, as well as the voraciousness with which TV had gone through the libraries of old movies. It, however, did not go beyond the first production, titled *Johnny North.* Television censors advised NBC that the film was far too rough and ugly. It was slated for release in theatres and retitled *The Killers* in an attempt to

With Angie Dickinson.

borrow on Ernest Hemingway's fame, although the connection between the author and this film is tenuous. Lew Wasserman, Reagan's agent during the actor's Warner years, had been made head of Universal. It was he who persuaded Reagan to accept the radical departure from his "nice guy" image, which Reagan claims to regret to this day.

The two killers of the 1964 version are Charlie (Lee Marvin) and Lee (Clu Gulager). They are commissioned to end the life of Johnny North (John Cassavetes), an ex-racing driver who now teaches in a school for the blind. After he is murdered, the thugs begin to wonder why their victim had shown no resistance and why anyone would pay $25,000 to have him killed. They learn that he had been involved in a million dollar robbery several years earlier, which then causes them to wonder what happened to the money. They begin to piece together the story from various people who knew North. He had been a successful racer until he fell in love with a beautiful girl called Sheila (Angie Dickinson), the mistress of a powerful underworld figure, Browning (Reagan). Following a crash, North returns to being a mechanic, but Sheila persuades him to take part in a major robbery as the getaway driver. Knowing that Browning will cheat them, North and Sheila plan to take off with the money. What he does not know until too late is that she has become Browning's wife, and is part of the crook's intended double-cross. However, the plans do not work out to anyone's satisfaction, and the main participants are killed.

This version of *The Killers* lacks the plausibility of the 1946 film and disperses its material in confusing plot shifts. Director Don Siegel deserves credit for pacing and the helicopter photography in the robbery sequence, but the film is defeated by its unpleasant tone. Most critics agreed that Ronald Reagan gave a convincing account of the brutal, coldly calculating crook but more than one felt that it was still difficult after so many years of seeing Reagan playing pleasant, moral, warm and civilized fellows to accept him as a villain, especially one who would slap a pretty girl like Angie Dickinson.

The Killers does not present a fitting finale to the film career of Ronald Reagan. But, then, it was not intended for the big screen of the theatres, only for the little one in the home. It is much better to remember him as the stalwart Commander Casey Abbott in *Hellcats of the Navy* or better still as George Gipp, Grover Cleveland Alexander or Drake McHugh of *Kings Row.*